Damselflies of the
North Woods

Damselflies
of the North Woods
By Bob DuBois

Kollath-Stensaas
PUBLISHING

Kollath-Stensaas Publishing
394 Lake Avenue South, Suite 406
Duluth, MN 55802
Office: 218.727.1731
Orders: 800.678.7006
sparkystensaas@hotmail.com

DAMSELFLIES *of the* NORTH WOODS

Printed in Duluth, Minnesota by Service Printers
10 9 8 7 6 5 4 3 2 1   First Edition

Editorial Director: Mark Sparky Stensaas
Graphic Designer: Rick Kollath

ISBN 0-9673793-7-7

North Woods Naturalist Guides from Kollath-Stensaas Publishing

Dragonflies of the North Woods
by Kurt Mead

Spiders of the North Woods
by Larry Weber

Butterflies of the North Woods
by Larry Weber

Butterflies of New England
by Larry Weber

Rock Picker's Guide to Lake Superior's North Shore
by Mark Sparky Stensaas & Rick Kollath

Wildflowers of the BWCA & North Shore
by Mark Sparky Stensaas & Rick Kollath

Table of Contents

To my wife Linda and daughters
Danielle, Christina and Sarah
And to my parents,
Robert P. and Malvina

Acknowledgements

I could not have written this book without the support of my family—the nucleus of people who make my life worthwhile. First, I thank my wife Linda, who has been a continual source of optimism and encouragement, and who has helped create time and space for me to pursue my passion for all things odonatological. My parents, Robert P. and Malvina DuBois, have enthusiastically supported and encouraged my interest in the natural world for the last 50 years or so. And to my daughters Danielle and Christina, thank you for joining me on collecting trips, and for patiently listening to far too many lengthy discourses on every conceivable topic related to the Odonata, and mostly just for being the incredible young women of faith and integrity that you are. And a big thanks to my diligent oldest daughter Sarah, who has encouraged me in my studies of the natural world from a distance—maybe one day we will be able to trek the fields and wetlands together in search of damselflies, eh Sarah?

I also want to acknowledge the help I've received in studying Odonata, and in many cases the friendships that have developed, from the following North Woods odonate enthusiasts: Matt Berg, Colin Jones, Karl Legler, Kurt Mead, Mark O'Brien, Julie Pleski, Mike Reese, Kurt Schmude, Wayne Steffens and Ken Tennessen. Special thanks to Bill Smith for being my always-cheerful Odonata mentor and to Nick Donnelly for patiently bearing with what must at times have seemed like an endless stream of distribution and taxonomic questions. I was fortunate to cross paths with a photographer with the talent of Mike Reese and with an illustrator with the skills of Rick Kollath. Sparky, thanks for being helpful and patient every step of the way.

Bob DuBois
May 14, 2005

We wish to thank Bob for his full involvement in this project. His enthusiasm for damselflies and dragonflies has rubbed off on many folks...including us! Many hours afield spent wandering and wading were required for the creation of this book. Dragonfly and damselfly expert Sid Dunkle double checked our facts and identifications. The damselfly photos by Mike Reese and Sid Dunkle really make this book something special. As always, editor Catherine Long kept the text clean and consistent. A big thanks to all.

The Publishers: Mark Sparky Stensaas, Rick Kollath
June 1, 2005

Parts of the Damselfly

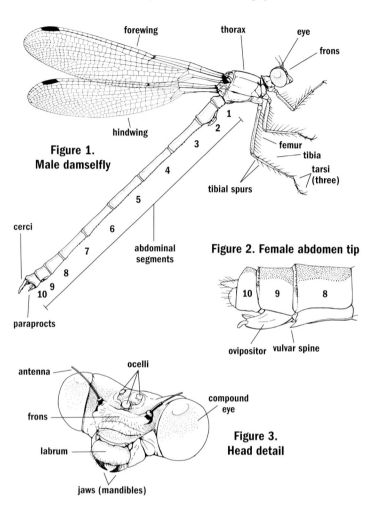

forewing

thorax

eye

frons

hindwing

**Figure 1.
Male damselfly**

1
2
3
4
5
6
7
8
9
10

femur

tibia

**tarsi
(three)**

tibial spurs

**abdominal
segments**

cerci

paraprocts

Figure 2. Female abdomen tip

10   9   8

ovipositor   **vulvar spine**

ocelli

antenna

**compound
eye**

frons

labrum

**Figure 3.
Head detail**

jaws (mandibles)

Figure 4. Wing detail

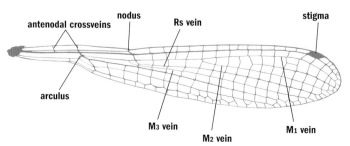

antenodal crossveins

nodus

Rs vein

stigma

arculus

M3 vein

M2 vein

M1 vein

What is a Damselfly?

Remember when you were in high school and you learned about the biological classification system developed by Carl Linnaeus in 1758? Big groups were at the top of the chart that steadily got smaller toward the bottom: phylum and class, then order and family, then finally, the most specific categories of genus and species. Well, if you had a good science teacher, she or he probably explained to you why this terrifically successful system has remained in wide use for so long (with many modifications). One of the big reasons is that it gives us a framework for wrapping our minds around the staggering complexity and diversity of life. Otherwise, there would just be an enormous number of different critters out there, some more similar to each other than others, but we would have no frame of reference for organizing and discussing this diversity. So, how do damselflies fit into this system?

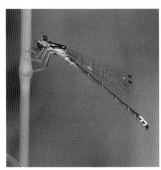

Damselflies, like this Eastern Forktail, tend to hold their wings together up over their back.

Damselflies are joint-legged arthropods (phylum Arthropoda) within the class Insecta (insects), within the order Odonata, which means "toothed" or "toothed ones" referring to the rapacious jaws of damselflies and dragonflies. The common name "damselfly" comes from the French word demoiselle meaning "young mistress." I like to think that this refers to the slender, graceful appearance of damselflies. Within the Odonata are two Suborders of significance to us: the dragonflies (Anisoptera) and the damselflies (Zygoptera). Many

Damselflies	Dragonflies
Eyes separated by at least own width	Eyes in contact with each other *(except clubtails)*
Hammer-headed, much wider than long	Bulbous-headed, nearly as long as wide
Long, slender build	Stout build
Weak, fluttery flight	Strong, sustained flight
Wings held over back when perched (or at 45 degree angle)	Wings held flat and perpendicular to body when perched.
Ovipositor present and functional	Ovipositor non-functional *(except in darners)*

people, myself included, use the term odonate ("ode" for short) when referring to both dragonflies and damselflies.

To clarify how the two groups differ, let's consider what their scientific names mean. Anisoptera means "unlike wings," referring to the hindwings of dragonflies being larger than the forewings and differently shaped. In damselflies, the forewings and hindwings are similar in size and shape. This similarity is alluded to in the name Zygoptera, which roughly translates to "paired wings," from the Greek term *zygon* meaning "yoke." As you might guess from being in the same order, dragonflies and damselflies have a whole lot in common in terms of basic body plan and even many behaviors including reproduction and feeding. However, note the wing shape and the differences shown on the chart on page 1 to help you separate them.

There are 19 families of damselflies worldwide containing over 2,500 named species. Many more species undoubtedly exist that have not yet been named, especially in the tropics. In North America north of Mexico we have five families with about 132 species. Here in the North Woods we have three families containing 46 species: four species of broad-winged damsels (Calopterygidae), nine species of spreadwings (Lestidae), and 33 species of pond damsels (Coenagrionidae). This total includes seven "borderline" species that rarely stray to the North Woods.

Damselfly Parts

The primary divisions of the damselfly's body are the head, thorax and abdomen. The head is much wider than long, with the large, compound eyes separated by a distance greater than the eye's width.

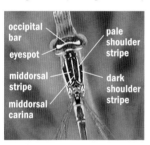

occipital bar
eyespot
middorsal stripe
middorsal carina
pale shoulder stripe
dark shoulder stripe

Knowing the head and thorax markings helps in identification.

This gives a damselfly a distinctly hammer-headed appearance. The huge compound eyes contain 5,000 to 10,000 individual light-sensitive units (**ommatidia**) and are well adapted for slow flight among vegetation and accurate perception of prey at short distances. It is not known if damselflies see color. Three simple eyes called **ocelli** are also found on top of the head. Many species have pale **eyespots**, (**postocular spots**) on top of the head that are useful in identification. These eyespots differ in size among species and may be connected by a pale, transverse line called the **occipital bar**. The head is hollowed out at the rear and loosely connected to the thorax so that it can rotate freely when scanning side-to-side and up and down in search of prey.

The **mouth** is a complex but efficient "team" of parts that work together to get prey into the stomach quickly. The uppermost mouthpart (**labrum**) and the lowermost mouthpart (**labium**) hold the prey securely so the inner jaws can do the chewing. The inner jaws are comprised of a pair of stout, wedge-shaped **mandibles**, that tackle most of the heavy duty chewing, and a pair of more slender **maxillae**. The **antennae** are small and bristle-like, composed of 6 or 7 segments.

The damselfly **thorax** is unique. The front section (**prothorax**) controls movement of the head and the front pair of legs. One of the signature features of damselflies is that the two rear thorax parts are fused together to form the box-like **pterothorax**. This powerful "wheelhouse" contains the all of the flight musculature, to which the wings are directly attached, and it controls movement of the two hind pairs of legs as well. The structure of the thorax is skewed such that the legs are thrust forward and the wings backward, which aids in the capture of aerial prey and the gleaning of prey from surfaces while damselflies are in flight.

The **wings** of damselflies are flexible membranous structures, laced with tubes called **veins** that lend strength to the wing while at the same time allowing flexibility. When perched, the wings of damselflies are usually held together vertically above the body. However, the spreadwings (genus *Lestes*) and the Aurora

A male American Rubyspot stops and rests on the wings of an egg-laying Ebony Jewelwing.

Damsel, rest with the wings partly spread at about a 45 degree angle to the body. Damselflies never hold their wings perpendicular to the body like an airplane, as dragonflies do.

Damselfly wings are directly attached to the muscles that move them, a condition called **paleopterous** (meaning ancient-winged). In contrast, most flying insects have the flight muscles directly attached only to the thorax and the wings move indirectly as a result of contraction of the thorax. This latter condition is called **neopterous** (meaning modern-winged) and permits more rapid wing movement. This is one of the reasons why a housefly can flap its wings many more times per second than a damselfly can. Damselflies lack a hinge at the wing base and therefore cannot fold their wings flat over their backs.

One prominent feature of the wing is the **stigma**, a darkened cell of uncertain function near the tip of each wing. What is certain is that the shape and color of the stigma is often useful in identification. All the wing veins of a damselfly—longitudinal veins, cross veins, and even some areas of vein intersection—have names and a thorough study of them takes time. But, learning just a few key veins and other wing parts (see pg. viii) will help immensely in identifying our northern damsels.

Like all insects, damselflies have six jointed-legs. The long, upper leg section near the body is the **femur**. The next long section in the middle is the **tibia**. And the **tarsi** are comprised of three small sections making up the "foot." Rows of spine-like **spurs** along the femur and tibia are useful in capturing prey.

The **abdomen** of a damselfly is slender, cylindrical and always has ten segments, numbered 1 through 10, starting at the thorax. Patterns of color on these segments are often vitally important in identification, so it is well worth learning how to count up from the base, or back from the tip, to find the segment in question. Segment 1 is usually very short, while segments 2 and 3 are longer and modified underneath in males to hold the secondary genitalia, a complex array of reproductive organs. In all Odonata, sperm is produced in testes near the tip of the abdomen at segment 9, but the male must transfer free sperm to his own secondary genitalia prior to mating. This need for a male to transfer sperm from one end of his abdomen to the other, is unique in the insect world. With his "tool kit" of reproductive parts the male is not only able to deliver his own sperm to the female, but he can also first remove any sperm of other males left from previous matings.

At the tip of the male's abdomen are a set of **claspers**, or **terminal appendages**, which are comprised of the upper pair (**cerci**) and the lower pair (**paraprocts**). The male uses his claspers to grasp the thorax of the female prior to mating. The tip of the female's abdomen also has pairs of cerci and paraprocts, but these are quite small and serve no known function in reproduction. The reproductive organs of the female consist of a genital aperture at the end of the segment 8, and a well-developed and fully functional ovipositor underneath segment 9. The **ovipositor** includes three sets of parts used to incise plant tissue and extrude one or several eggs into each cut. The shape and size of the ovipositor, and the presence or absence of a **vulvar spine** on the underside of segment 8, are useful aids in identification. This discussion of the abdomen reminds me of the story of the young lad, who, asked by his teacher what the abdomen was used for, replied, "it contains the bowels, of which there are five—A, E, I, O and U!"

Biology & Behavior 101

The life cycle of a damselfly includes a lengthy aquatic stage as a larva, often a year or more in duration, followed by a quick and absolutely stunning transformation into a winged adult. Despite their apparently gentle and serene demeanor, damselflies are ferociously predatory during both stages of life. In the long, slow larval stage, the goal is pretty much just to grow. During the brief, but frenetic, adult stage, the primary goal is to reproduce. But to reproduce effectively, young adults must feed, gain weight and mature sexually, before they are ready to undergo the rigors of defending territories and competing for mates. Let's take a closer look at how this happens, first by peeking inside the bedroom door.

Mating

Damselflies mate only as mature adults. The required maturation period lasts from a day to several weeks, and usually takes place away from the breeding site, often in nearby clearings and forest edges depending on species. When ready to mate, males congregate at rendezvous sites at or near the breeding areas where they space themselves to await the arrival of females. Males of some North Woods species, including the jewelwings (genus *Calopteryx*) and some dancers (genus *Argia*), will actively defend territories from other males, as do many dragonflies. Most of our species are not aggressively territorial, though when two male forktails (genus *Ischnura*) interact, one may chase the other from the rendezvous site. Males of some

A male River Jewelwing courts a nearby female with his wing display.

of our species wait well inland where they attempt to intercept females before they reach the rendezvous sites. Hagen's Bluet is known to employ this sly tactic. Males of other species will patrol for females along pond edges without being territorial or engaging in aggressive behavior with other males. As a rule, females arrive at rendezvous or breeding sites after the males and only when ready to mate.

Before mating, the male must transfer free sperm from his testes on abdominal segment 9 to his secondary genitalia on abdominal segments 2 and 3. To do this he arches his abdomen until the appropriate segments meet. Fully loaded, he is now ready to initiate what is easily one of the most amazing spectacles in the insect world — formation of the **mating wheel**. The male uses his claspers to unceremoniously grab a female by the thorax. The pair is now **"in tandem"** and fly to a nearby perch. If she is ready to mate, she curls her abdomen forward so that the genital opening at the end of her abdomen engages the male's secondary genitalia. This produces a heart-shaped or circular configuration of their bodies commonly called being **"in wheel"** or **"in copula."** Copulation then proceeds for several minutes on average, most of this time being used by the male to remove any sperm of males that may have previously mated with that female. During the last few seconds of copulation, he transfers his own sperm into her sac-like **bursa** where it is stored until she actually lays her eggs.

A pair of Spotted Spreadwings in a "mating wheel," the heart-shaped position is typical of damselflies.

Mating between different species (**hybridization**) rarely occurs because a proper fit of the male's claspers with the female's thoracic plates is necessary for tandem formation. However, male pond damsels can be shockingly undiscriminating, and may attempt to take in-tandem females of any species approaching the right size. Happily, females have patterns of sensory areas on their thorax that match the shape of the male's claspers. This allows them to correctly identify males of their species and reject imposters.

Egg-laying and Guarding

After mating, the male may leave immediately so that the female lays the eggs alone, or he may guard the female while she deposits the eggs. Two forms of **guarding** are used by North Woods damselflies. The males of the broad-winged damsels release the female, but fly with her to the egg-laying site where he guards by hovering or perching nearby (**non-contact guarding**). In this strategy, he chases away competing males that attempt to mate with the egg-laying female, and he remains free to mate with other nearby females himself. By far the most common strategy for North Woods species is for the male to remain in tandem while the female deposits her eggs (**contact guarding**). Either form of guarding enables the male to protect his genetic investment from being removed by competing males, and it allows the female to deposit eggs without being unduly harassed by other males. Females of most species mate repeatedly during the several weeks of their adult life. In a few species, notably our forktails, a single mating is apparently the rule.

Female damselflies use their ovipositors to deposit eggs directly into the stems of rushes and sedges, into clumps of moss or into pieces of floating plant material. The female uses her blade-like ovipositor to "saw" punctures into the plant tissue (either above or below water) and extrude one or several eggs into each puncture. This egg-laying process is called **oviposition**. Females of species that lay eggs underwater may descend a foot or more and remain submerged for over one hour! Their supply of oxygen comes from a

A single male Ebony Jewelwing watches over a bunch of females laying eggs. This is called non-contact guarding. Note his black wings that lack a white spot at the tip.

thin film of air that adheres to hairs on the body surface. Contact-guarding males may get dragged, kicking and screaming I imagine, partially or wholly under water as well, although they usually release their grip before their head gets pulled under. Females of most pond damsels (family Coenagrionidae) rest horizontally on floating plant leaves when depositing eggs with the contact-guarding male standing rigidly upright as if "at attention," supported only by the grasp of his claspers on her thorax. I must confess that seeing males in this **"sentinel" position** often strikes me as

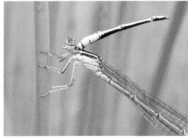

It is not uncommon for a male's abdomen to break off while in-tandem with a female, perhaps during the attack of a predator.

amusing, although I doubt I could explain why. Occasionally, due to a predator attack, the abdomen of the male breaks off in this position, leaving the lower part still attached to the female and sticking straight up. Ouch! First time I ever saw this, my initial thought was that I had witnessed some type of ghastly damselfly deformity.

The Aquatic Larval Stage

Damselflies spend the majority of their lives as slender, greenish or brownish, rather nondescript larvae, crawling around underwater hunting their prey. They live in nearly every imaginable type of freshwater habitat including rivers, streams, lakes, ponds, vernal (temporary) pools, marshes, swamps, bogs, fens and spring seeps. The great majority of our species are found in still-water habitats, with very few found in rapid streams. Damselfly larvae differ from dragonfly larvae in several ways. They are more slender, and the head is wider than the thorax or abdomen. Three, slender-leaf-shape "gills" (**caudal lamellae**) at the tip of the abdomen help them breathe under water.

Damselfly larvae are slender and long-bodied compared to the bulky, oval larvae of their cousins the dragonflies.

The elongate eggs hatch rather quickly, usually from 12 days to five weeks after being laid, depending on air and water temperature, season and species. The eggs of spreadwings overwinter. When an egg hatches, a tiny prolarva is released. Within just seconds or minutes, the exoskeleton of the prolarva is rent apart and the first true larval stage bursts forth. Because the larval exoskeleton has little elasticity, the only way for the larva to grow is to shed the old skin and replace it with a slightly larger one. As the larvae feed and grow, North Woods species progress through from ten to 17 molts before they are ready to transform into adults. Each period between molts is called an **instar**.

Tireless hunters, larval damselflies lurk on stems of standing aquatic plants or in beds of submersed vegetation, actively pursuing smaller insect prey or even tiny fish. To grab their prey, they are equipped with an elongate, hinged jaw (**labium**), which they are able to extend out with lightning speed, latching onto the prey with their raptorial labial hooks. Like so many things peculiar to the Odonata, this highly modified mouthpart seems to be unique in the insect world. Although capable of striking fear into the hearts of a vast array of small aquatic critters, larval damselflies do not bite or harm humans in any way.

While obtaining dinner is important to a larval damselfly's survival, avoiding being dinner for some scary creature larger than itself is clearly a priority as well. Many animals dine on larval damselflies, including water birds, sunfishes, black bass and their own cousins, the larval dragonflies. Ingenious studies by Mark McPeek of Dartmouth and colleagues have shown that ponds with sunfishes and black bass tend to have different damselfly species than fishless ponds. It turns out that some species of damselfly larvae try to escape from predators by swimming away, while others are content to crawl away and hide. The strategy of swimming away works well when escaping from insect predators, but not so well when the predators are fish. Pretty cool stuff, eh?

The larval stage typically lasts a year but sometimes up to three years. A general rule is that larger species, and species living in more northerly environs, take longer to develop. Most of our species over-winter as larvae, except for spread-wings, the majority of which over-winter in the egg stage. Two of our Eurasian bluets (Taiga Bluet and Prairie Bluet) are known to over-winter actually embedded in ice! Some species of our spreadwings

Lyre-tipped Spreadwings depositing eggs into the stem of a rush as the males continue to guard their females.

are adapted to live in temporary ponds; in these species the larval stage may be completed in five months or less, before the ponds dry up.

Emergence

After months or years of clambering about underwater, the larva is freed from the shackles of this ignoble existence in one grand moment of emancipation. Almost instantly it becomes one of the most graceful and elegant flying creatures under the sun. In the days before this transformation the larva goes through many changes; it turns darker, becomes more sluggish, stops feeding and the wing pads begin to swell. The larval mouthparts and other larval structures become dysfunctional because the new adult (**pharate adult**) is now forming while imprisoned inside the **larval exoskeleton**. Just before emergence, the larva rests at the water's surface with head and part of the thorax exposed and begins breathing through spiracles that have opened up on the sides of the thorax.

Unlike dragonflies, which often emerge at night or during the early morning, most damselflies emerge later in the morning or during midday. Nearly all our species climb a few inches above the water's surface on aquatic plant stems and emerge in a vertical position. A few species of dancers climb onto logs or rocks and may emerge in a horizontal position. To begin emergence, the larva gains a secure grip on the emergence perch with its **tarsal claws** and rests for a few minutes while drying off. Then the thorax begins to bulge and splits longitudinally along its top. The top of the head also splits from side to side. These splits meet and then the thorax of the new adult, followed by its head, push out from this opening in the larval skin (**exuviae**). Now free, the head and the thorax hang backwards for a few minutes while the new exoskeleton and the legs begin to

A trio of Sweetflag Spreadwings (two males (above) and a female (below) temporarily left hanging). This is likely the top male's attempt to foil the other male's mating success.

harden. When the legs are strong enough, the new adult suddenly bends forward and grasps the emergence perch or its own exuviae and pulls out its abdomen. The abdomen extends with air pressure from the gut and the wings unfurl and expand as blood (**hemolymph**) is pumped into them. Full expansion of the wings and abdomen takes up to an hour before flight can be attempted.

The newly emerged damselfly, now called a **teneral**, is pale yellow in color with no dark markings. Tenerals gain color quickly, but most species don't acquire full adult coloration until at least a few days after emergence.

Initially the flight is feeble and the wings glisten and shimmer in the sun. It is now very vulnerable to predation by birds, frogs, spiders, predatory insects and even carnivorous plants like sundews. First flights are away from water as the tenerals scatter from the breeding site to feed and gain strength in nearby clearings, meadows and forest edges.

Damselflies are not as overtly migratory as are some species of dragonflies. Nonetheless, dispersal is an important facet of the ecology of many damselfly species. **Dispersal** just means flying to find new breeding sites rather than remaining at the old one. Most of our species disperse to at least some extent, some specifically to colonize newly created or temporary habitats, others to seek areas of less intense competition for resources and mates. The period when tenerals scatter from the breeding site is a major time of dispersal for damselflies. In the North Woods, the Familiar Bluet is a notable disperser. I have seen bogs and fens in northern Wisconsin that were densely populated with tenerals of this species in early September become totally devoid of any individuals just a week or two later.

Tiny damselflies are not babies, they are simply fully grown adults of small species. The cast skin, or exuviae, remains on the emergence perch, usually a plant stem, until it is carried away by wind, rain or high water. The exuviae retains the form of the mature larva very well, and for that reason, can often be identified to species using larval keys. Emergence of all individuals of a species usually occurs over a two to three week period, although some forktails (genus *Ischnura*) extend emergence over several months.

Coloration

One of the reasons why damselflies are so enjoyable to watch is that they come in such a striking variety of colors—beautiful blues, often with contrasting black markings, and iridescent greens are common. Other North Woods species display various hues of yellow, orange, red, purple and brown. Colors and patterns play a huge role in identifying all our species. Patterns of coloration that contrast with the surrounding areas come in the form of stripes (narrow and elongate, running with the body), spots (roundish and usually small), and transverse bands (often called rings or annuli if they encircle a structure).

Learning to recognize our 46 species by colors and patterns is a bit more challenging than would initially appear. This is because males and females often do not look alike (**sexual dichromatism**). Also, tenerals of all species are much paler than mature adults, and lack dark markings. Male pond damsels are usually more brightly colored than their females. Identifying females to species can be quite tricky as there can be male-like forms and species that become grayish or bluish as they age (**pruinescence**). Pruinosity is a waxy substance that exudes from the cuticle. It is not limited to females; in spreadwings it is most pronounced in males. Male Powdered Dancers become quite pruinose as they age. The bright blues of some pond damsels can change to dull purple in response to temperature changes or darkness.

Parasitism

As you begin to observe damselflies closely you will soon notice that many have small orange or red egg-like bodies attached to the underside of their thorax or abdomen. These are not damselfly eggs but rather water mite parasites that settle on the damselfly when in the larval stage. When the damselfly larva emerges, the larval mite is able to quickly crawl off the exuviae and transfer his boarding pass to the teneral damselfly. The mite now begins the parasitic stage, attaching to the new adult damselfly and sucking its body fluids for at least three or four weeks. It will then drop off back into the water to complete its life cycle. Parasites do not usually kill their hosts, but a heavy parasite load may hamper a damselfly's feeding and reproductive success.

Feeding and Flight

Adult damselflies feed in two ways, the most common being the capture of flying insect prey on the wing using their forward-facing and spur-adorned legs kind of like a net. Some species also feed by gleaning small insect prey off the surfaces of foliage. Forktails are

especially good at gleaning. Damselflies feed opportunistically on whatever prey species are available, showing little selectivity for particular prey. A wide variety of flies are often the staple, with side dishes of caddisflies, small moths and other insects. Damselflies will certainly eat mosquitoes when they are available, but it is doubtful that they take enough to noticeably reduce populations. Once secured, the prey is carried to a nearby perch

Though dainty in appearance, damselflies are capable of taking substantial prey items like this moth.

and rapidly consumed in rather large chunks. Contrary to the beliefs of some, damselflies neither sting nor bite hard enough to cause any serious pain to humans.

It is the remarkable and complex flying ability of damselflies that allows them to be very effective aerial predators. Although lacking the blazing speed of their larger cousins the dragonflies, damselflies excel at being quick, precise and extraordinarily maneuverable. They can fly in virtually any direction, even straight backwards. Their forewings and hind wings usually beat about 180 degrees out of phase, but they can also move all four wings synchronously or all four wings at different rates. Damselflies possess several flight advantages over other insects including an unusually high ratio of flight

A Mallard duckling happily pursues a bluet for lunch.

muscle to body mass and very low wing loading (the ratio of body mass to wing area). They are best suited to foraging low and slowly among vegetation, where their excellent vision allows them to home in on small prey at short distances. The habit of most damselflies to fly low, both amongst vegetation and over water, probably serves to reduce the risk of their being eaten by birds.

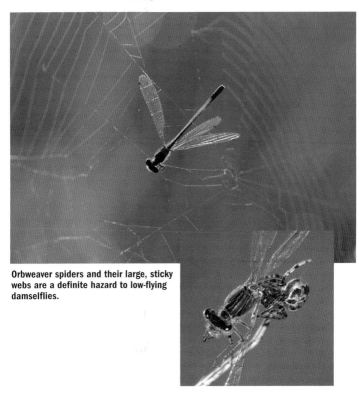

Orbweaver spiders and their large, sticky webs are a definite hazard to low-flying damselflies.

Damselfly Observation

Why watch damselflies? Well, there are a bunch of good reasons, but among the best are that they are beautiful little creatures, fascinating in their behaviors, and unlike so many other animals they are often easy to approach. Most species will offer the patient and careful observer a thorough look at all their sundry activities. Happily,

most damselflies are active right when many of us like to be out and about—late mornings and afternoons on sunny, warm days. I like the way Kurt Mead put it in *Dragonflies of the North Woods*, "the best time for dragonfly observation usually occurs after a long, late breakfast, complete with an extra cup of coffee." Exactly so with damselflies as well! A few of our species are crepuscular, meaning they fly until dusk or later.

For the beginner, a good way to get started in damselflying is simply to pull on a pair of boots, grab this field guide and head out to a nearby pond shoreline or other wetland on a sunny afternoon. Try to keep it simple

Amber-winged Spreadwings in-tandem communally deposit eggs into a rush stem.

and just enjoy the pleasures of discovery and exploration! Don't be afraid to hop right into their habitats. It is much more satisfying to immerse yourself in the damselfly's world than just watching their behavior from a distance. Perhaps the best tip I can give you is move slowly and pause often. You'll see much more that way. Observe the colors, sizes, behaviors and habitats of the damselflies you see flitting about you. Try to guess what they're doing and why. See if you can tell what family or genus they belong to. If you enjoy photography, you may want to learn how to photograph your tiny subjects.

Habitats and Seasons

Damselflies can be found just about anywhere, particularly right after emergence when they scatter from breeding sites. But your best chance of finding lots of action is to go to favorite breeding areas. Well-vegetated pond and lake shorelines will reliably harbor a good number of species. Sedge Sprites, spreadwings, bluets and forktails are often found in these areas. Marshes and swamps may also hold many species of the same groups. Rivers and streams have different and fewer species than do still-water habitats. But don't miss out on flowing-water habitats because the species there are strikingly colored and absorbing to watch. Look for jewelwings, dancers, red damsels, a few species of bluets and Aurora Damsels along rivers and streams. Bogs and fens will often have sprites, some spreadwings and a few species of bluets.

A number of species will be active each month from late May through early October in the North Woods, however, the group of species present in the spring will be vastly different than those in the autumn. A few species (notably the forktails) have long flight periods that span much of the flight season, but most species have peaks of activity for only a month or two. Early-sea-

Rest stop. A small fly has landed on the convenient abdomen of a perched Amber-winged Spreadwing.

son flyers include the jewelwings, the Eurasian bluets, and some of the American bluets (genus *Enallagma*). Late spring and summer groups include the rubyspots, a few spreadwings, the dancers, most American bluets, some forktails and the sprites. Classic late-season flyers include most spreadwings and some forktails, with the Spotted Spreadwing invariably being the latest.

Gear and Equipment

Earlier I advised you to try to keep it simple—for a good reason: you will be more relaxed and enjoy your outings more if you're not trying to accomplish too much at the outset. You will need a few tools. At the very top of the list should be a good pair of close-focusing binoculars. The key word here for successful damselflying is "close." Many companies now make models that can focus down to six feet or less. My pair easily focuses on my boot tops—while I'm wearing them! It is difficult to overstate how helpful a pair of good binocs can be. A full explanation of binocular features and a buyer's guide with specs on more than 38 models are found in Appendix E.

I urge you to consider keeping field notes of your outings. Doing so will help you learn to identify and know the habits of the species in your area more quickly. Taking notes is really quite enjoyable and will add richness to your outings. From May through October, I rarely go anywhere without my field notebook. It's even in the car on Sunday mornings when I'm on the way to church! You just never know when you're going to see something interesting. The most important things to record along with the species seen are the dates and locations where you found them. Locations should be described as precisely as possible, because if you find a rare species, other people will want to know where to look. Other things you may want to record are time of day, weather conditions, behaviors, life stages, evidence of breeding and habitat notes, including vegetation if you know something about it. If you keep up with your notes diligently, over time they will become increasingly valuable both to you and from a scientific perspective. People who work with dragonflies and damselflies professionally are quick to affirm that citizen enthusiasts have greatly increased scientific knowledge about species distributions, habitats and behaviors. Any small notebook will do, but many people prefer Rite-in-the-Rain-type notebooks because they have waterproof paper. Always use pencil because ink may run when wet.

This male Tule Bluet is alertly defending his female as she lays eggs. This behavior is called contact-guarding and he is in the "sentinel" position

Proper dress is important to an enjoyable outing, including sunscreen and bug juice when appropriate. I like to wear a hat with a wide brim, lightweight field clothing and breathable waders that are scarcely heavier than slacks. I use hip-high or chest-high waders depending on the water depth where I'm going. Some folks are perfectly happy just to wet-wade in tennis shoes—which is fine for them, just don't ask me to do it! Knee-high boots will suffice in many situations, but don't be surprised if you go over the tops. A canoe or other small boat can get you to deep or muck-bottomed areas that would be impossible or unpleasant to wade to, but be careful— swinging a net from a canoe is tricky business, unless you enjoy swimming.

Gaining access to good sites for damselflying can require a bit of planning. If you want access to private property, be sure to ask permission of the landowner first. When in doubt, ask—it's better to be safe than sorry. Depending on ownership, different public properties have different rules about public access and about the activities that are permissible on the property. To see detailed written guidance for property access in Wisconsin, go to the Wisconsin Odonata Survey website (http://atriweb.info/inventory/odonata). Property access requirements in other states and Canada may differ—be sure you do your homework.

Nets and Netting

If being able to identify all damselflies to species is important to you, then you'll want to get a net. To identify many species, you must examine small body parts under magnification. Netting is the best way to get them into your possession. Unlike many dragonflies, damselflies are usually easy to net. Of course, there will be exceptions, and the exceptions will be the ones you really need to see up close!

If a damselfly is perched high on a twig or flying, swing the net through the damselfly just like you would swing a bat through a pitched softball. Unlike dragonflies, which usually must be netted from behind or below because of their lightning quick evasiveness, most flying damselflies can be netted from any direction with a reasonably quick stroke.

Most damselflies regularly perch on vegetation near the ground, so simply approach them quietly and deliberately, and quickly drop your net over the top of them. Then, leaving the frame of the net down, hold the tip of the netting up, so the netting looks like a giant upside-down ice cream cone. Damselflies will invariably fly upward at this point, towards the tip of the cone. Keeping the net rim

A vulnerable position. This male Stream Bluet is still contact-guarding his mate, though she has descended underwater to deposit eggs into an aquatic plant stem. I wonder if he's getting a bit nervous?

low, reach your hand under the rim and up into the cone to grasp the damselfly. Using your index and middle fingers, grasp the four wings together over its back and carefully remove it from the net. The closer to the base you hold the wings, the less likely you are to

break any of them. Now you can examine it with a hand lens or pre-
pare it to bring home to examine under a microscope. Very small
species must be handled with great care to avoid injuring them, and
tenerals should not be handled as they almost certainly will be dam-
aged. Most mature damselflies that are netted in the way just
described can be released unharmed.

Look for a net with a deep bag, a rim with an opening of at least
15 inches and a lightweight handle at least three feet long. Some nets
come with extendable handles, allowing you to add segments to get
any length you want. Others are collapsible for easy travel. Bear in
mind that a longer, heavier net is harder to swing quickly, and
swinging quickly is really the key. Most people find that a net with
an 18-inch rim works well. Children do best with a smaller net. I
often use a net with a 21-inch rim because I have arms like a gorilla.
Just kidding. Truth is, I appreciate the greater "margin for error"
afforded by a larger rim because I chase dragonflies with the same
net. Nets can be homemade or purchased from a number of equipment sources. BioQuip Products stocks a variety of net sizes and
styles and also sells replacement bags.

Collecting

Although not for everyone, some damselfly enthusiasts choose to
maintain a collection of these insects. Most scientists who study
damselflies do so of necessity as well. The reasons for collecting specimens are many. Collected specimens, properly curated, are permanent and verifiable records of species distributions. It is important to
document these distributions because they can change over time in
response to losses of habitat, influences of invasive species and other

A pair of Violet Dancers laying eggs with Stream Bluets at a communal ovipositing site.

factors. Management agencies charged with the responsibility of conserving and protecting natural resources for future generations need to know what species occur in different areas and what habitats are critical to their survival. Many state and provincial agencies now use citizen volunteers in surveys to help determine distributions and critical habitats of species (see Appendix B for information about surveys in Ontario, Michigan and Wisconsin). Usually, some collecting is required to contribute to these surveys in a meaningful way.

For some species, collection is necessary because careful examination under a microscope is the only way to identify them with certainty. Reference specimens are crucial for scientists who study identification and the phylogenetic relationships of species. Specimens are needed to properly determine relationships of closely related species and groups. Besides being essential to research, collecting specimens can be a source of pleasure and education. Responsible collecting poses no threat to damselfly populations, although restrictions on collecting are appropriate when populations are dangerously low, habitats are especially fragile or legal reasons apply.

In sum, collecting is a great way to learn, and it is a crucial tool in the protection and conservation of damselflies. If you are thinking about starting a collection, you should first read the *Responsible Collecting Guidelines* put out by the World Dragonfly Association and the Dragonfly Society of the Americas on their websites (see Appendix B). Then learn the proper techniques for collecting, preserving and storing specimens, also from these websites.

Equipment Sources

BioQuip Products: A wide selection of aerial nets (including the popular collapsible net), aquatic nets, Odonata envelopes, field guides, scopes and other entomological equipment. www.bioquip.com 310.667.8800

Acorn Naturalists: A great source for aquatic dip nets, books and other naturalist and teaching resources. www.acornnaturalists.com 800.422.8886

International Odonatological Research Institute: Best source for collecting envelopes. Also field guides and other books. http://www.afn.org/~iori/

How to use this Field Guide

Damselflies of the North Woods is designed to make field identification easier for you, the reader. Through the use of color photos, arrows pointing to field marks, size scales, phenograms and habitats, we have made a handy, compact and easy to use guide. Also, by limiting the damselflies to those found in one geographic area, we have eliminated the need to wade through several hundred species, many of which would never be found here. Included is every regularly occurring damselfly in the North Woods of the Western Great Lakes.

Order

Damselflies are organized by families and then broken down further into genera. Family name is listed at the bottom of the left page of each species spread while the genus is listed on the bottom of the right page. We placed closely related species next to each other. With experience in the field using this guide, you will gradually learn to identify damselflies to family, then genus and eventually, species.

Damselfly Names

Like other organisms, damselflies are given both common and scientific names. The common names are the English names most amateur naturalists use, while the scientific or Latin names tend to be the spoken word of odonatists. We capitalize species names but use lower case for groups (e.g. Stream Bluets are actually a type of bluet).

Photos

We chose to use photos of free-flying damselflies in their natural habitat. Males are always pictured on the left page of the spread and, with only a few exceptions, females are pictured on the right. The symbol used for males is ♂ and the female symbol is ♀. Photo credits are listed in Appendix C.

Abundance

A blue circle on each photo shows the relative abundance of each species: A=abundant, C=common, FC=fairly common, O=occasional, U=uncommon, R=rare and VR=very rare. Of course, even a "rare" species may be locally common if you happen to be in their preferred habitat at the right time.

Fieldmark Arrows

Arrows point to diagnostic features in the photos that are referenced in the description text and marked with an arrow symbol (↑). These are characteristics that you should look for while in the field. Jotting down notes on size, color, thoracic stripes, abdomen markings and wing features will help you identify the damselfly when you have a chance to consult this book.

Size Scale

Size is relative and often hard to judge in the field. Use the size-bars at the top of each species' main photo. The black bar indicates the actual body length of that species.

Phenograms

What is a phenogram? All damselflies live out their lives according to seasonal timing that is characteristic for that species. Our phenogram highlights in red the time when that species is active as a flying adult. In other words, look for that damselfly during the highlighted weeks/months. Of course, weather and latitude will cause some variation in emergence dates and flight period.

Blue buttons estimate the relative abundance of that species.

The red phenogram indicates when you are most likely to see that damselfly on the wing.

Black size-bar indicates actual body length for the species.

Photo on the right side of the spread typically shows an adult female.

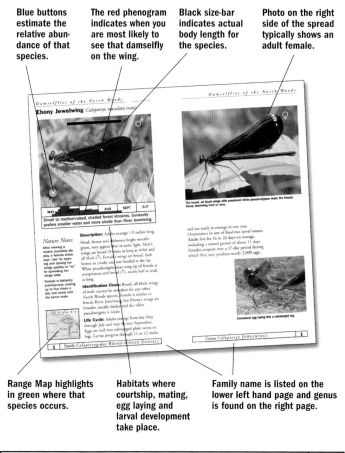

Range Map highlights in green where that species occurs.

Habitats where courtship, mating, egg laying and larval development take place.

Family name is listed on the lower left hand page and genus is found on the right page.

Habitat

Preferred habitat is found beneath the phenogram. Remember, this is where courtship, mating and egg laying takes place, and the larva develops and emerges. Your best bet to find the species will probably be near such habitats—but not exclusively. Damselflies can range widely over many different habitats.

Nature Notes

Nature Notes are fascinating bits of natural history that bring one a more complete understanding of that species. Unique behavior, population trends and naming history are just some of the topics touched on.

Range Map

A map of the North Woods shows the range of that species in green. This is the range as we know it from current population data but some damselfly populations are poorly understood.

☐ **Species Range**

Species Text

Description covers the best distinguishing characteristics first—whether it is the abdomen markings, shoulder stripes, wing color, veins or eyespots. If males and females are different (sexual dimorphism) then these differences are described. Measurements given are the average body length in inches.

Under **Identification Clues**, tips are given on how to separate that species from other similar damsels. Details of spreadwing male claspers (terminal appendages) and female ovipositors are shown side-by-side on page 37. Details of pond damsel male claspers are shown on pages 58-59. These features usually require a hand lens to see clearly.

Life Cycle covers flight season, courtship, male guarding, egg laying technique and larval development.

Glossary

Check out the glossary for easy-to-understand meanings of some tricky terms.

North Woods Damselfly Checklist

In Appendix A you will find a checklist of all 46 species found in the North Woods of Minnesota, Wisconsin, Michigan and northwest Ontario. Check off the ones you see in your travels afield.

Damselfly Groups & Websites

Damselfly and dragonfly organizations usually have websites that are fantastic sources of information. Appendix B.

Titles of Interest

This list of recommended reading and resources includes our favorite titles for delving deeper into the fascinating world of our "fair damsels." Also listed are books on close-up nature photography. Appendix D.

Binoculars for Damselflying

Recommended binoculars are those that focus close and are of good quality. Check out Appendix E if you are in the market for new "glass."

Enjoy *Damselflies of the North Woods*. Take it with on hikes. Stuff it in your canoe pack. Use it. But most importantly, have fun getting to know our fascinating northern damselflies.

Damselfly Identification

Just about any damselfly can be identified with enough effort, but some are easier than others. Unless you love a challenge, I suggest you focus your beginning efforts on the easier ones first and leave the others alone for a while. For example, as a rule, males are easier than females and mature adults are easier than tenerals. Of course, every rule has its exception. For example, because of her outrageously long ovipositor, the female Sweetflag Spreadwing is easier to identify than the male. Circumstances occur where even specialists may not attempt to identify every damselfly they see, especially some teneral females, because the difficulty and uncertainty of the result may simply not be worth the effort. Females can often be tentatively identified by identifying the males they are associating with.

Three levels of identification are typically used with damselflies: in-the-field, in-the-hand and under-a-microscope. In-the-field refers to species that can be identified by field markings with the naked eye or close-focusing binoculars. In-the-hand refers to species that must be captured and examined more closely because the body parts or marks used for identification are too small to be seen at a distance. For this level of identification I normally use a 16x hand lens. Under-a-microscope refers to identifications that can only be reliably made with magnification of greater than 20x (often at least 40x) and preferably with a specimen that is not moving (i.e. dead).

Damselflies of the North Woods will enable you to identify damselflies in-the-field and in-the-hand. First, compare the size, color, patterns and wing markings of the species in the field with the pictures in this guide. For broad-winged damsels, this step should be sufficient to identify them. For spreadwings and pond damsels, capture some males with your net and examine their terminal appendages with a hand lens, comparing them with the drawings in this guide. Also notice the patterns of stripes, spots and rings. First determine if the specimen is a spreadwing or a pond damsel using the Family Key on the opposite page. Spreadwings hold their wings partially open at rest, are larger and often are pruinose at the tip of the abdomen. Once you have your choice narrowed down to a group of species, use the identification clues given in the species accounts to rule out similar species. In this way, you can use this guide to identify mature males of virtually all of our species and about 70 percent of our females. This level of success represents what I believe is reasonably achievable for most nature enthusiasts. The under-a-microscope level is not addressed in this guide.

Family Key for adult North Woods Damselflies

1a. Wings colored with black, brown or red, with no "stalk" at the base and with many antenodal cross veins (see drawing below); body metallic green or bronze; large species: BROAD-WINGED DAMSEL of FAMILY CALOPTERYGIDAE (pg. 26)

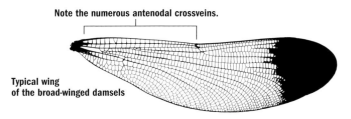

Note the numerous antenodal crossveins.

Typical wing
of the broad-winged damsels

1b. Wings clear or lightly colored with amber, with a distinct "stalk" at the base and with just two antenodal cross veins; body may be any color; large and small species: go to 2

2a. Wings held partially open at rest; wing median vein splits closer to the arculus than the nodus (see drawing below); mostly larger species: SPREADWING of FAMILY LESTIDAE (pg. 34)

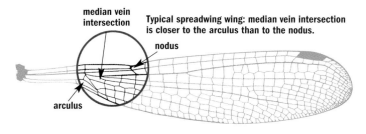

median vein
intersection

Typical spreadwing wing: median vein intersection
is closer to the arculus than to the nodus.

nodus

arculus

2b. Wings held together over the abdomen at rest (except Aurora Damsel); wing median vein splits closer to the nodus than the arculus (see drawing below); mostly smaller species: POND DAMSEL of FAMILY COENAGRIONIDAE (pg. 56)

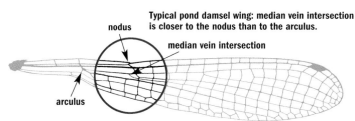

Typical pond damsel wing: median vein intersection
is closer to the nodus than to the arculus.

nodus

median vein intersection

arculus

Broad-winged Damselflies Family Calopterygidae

The broad-winged damsels are a small group of large, showy species that exclusively inhabit the flowing waters of rivers and streams. Some species prefer small to medium-sized streams, while others inhabit larger, slower rivers. They are readily separated from our other families of damselflies by easily seen characteristics of the wing, including color pattern, shape and wing venation. The family name, Calopterygidae, means "beautiful wing," referring to the strik-ing patterns of wing coloration in all of our species. Wing shape in this family differs from other families in that both wings are broad and lack a distinctly narrowed stalk at the base. Among the many wing venation characteristics peculiar to the group is the presence of many antenodal crossveins on each wing, whereas other families only have two antenodal crossveins per wing.

All males of our broad-winged species engage in showy courtship displays and defend small territories along the stream's edge. At the breeding sites, females match males in numbers, unusual among the damselflies. Females exercise choice in whether to accept or reject a displaying male. Eggs are deposited into plant stems that are often well below the water's surface. Males do not remain in tandem dur-ing oviposition, but rather, guard in non-contact fashion by hovering or perching nearby.

The larval stage lasts for at least a year and probably two or even three years for the River Jewelwing. The larvae crawl about on sub-merged roots, plant stems and other forms of vegetation along the edges of flowing waters. Not surprisingly, the larvae are large for damselflies and have broad wing pads. Larvae in this family are easily identified to species by characteristics of the labium, the length of antennal segments and presence or absence of abdominal spines.

At least 180 species of broad-winged damsels are known worldwide (mostly tropical), with only nine species found in North America. Here in the North Woods we have four species in two genera. Both sexes of all of our species are easily identified in the field by wing shape and color patterns.

The Jewelwings — Genus *Calopteryx*

The jewelwings are so named for the many species that have iri-descent wings. Our two species have wings that are either partially or wholly black and the females show bright white patches (pseudostig-mas) at the tips of their wings. Both genders lack true stigmas. Their bodies are a brilliant, metallic green, with blue reflections in some light. Both species have legs that are long, slender and dark. Jewelwings are the only North Woods damselflies with extensively black wings. Use the amount of black on the wings and wing shape to separate the two species.

Male jewelwings vigorously defend their "turf" along the edge of a stream, chasing away other males. In their territories they perform elaborate courtship displays, featuring special wing movements (see photo on pg. 5). If a female is receptive, she may allow the male to land on her closed wings, at which time he walks up along the wing's leading edge before taking her in tandem. To reject the male's display, the female simply spreads her wings and curves her abdomen up.

Virtually all writings on this genus have described the flight of jewelwings as bouncy and butterfly-like. Seeking fresh insights before writing this book, I spent extra time by my favorite jewelwing streams observing their behavior. I'm happy to report that their flight is bouncy and butterfly-like. You try coming up with a better description!

The Rubyspots — Genus *Hetaerina*

This genus gets its name from the unmistakable, blood red patches at the bases of the wings of males. The scientific name means "little companion," which Dennis Paulson and Sid Dunkle suggest may refer to the red armbands of Greek courtesans. The wings have venation patterns that are similar to our jewelwings but are a bit narrower, usually have a small stigma and lack extensive areas of black. The bodies of both genders are mostly bronze. Males perform courtship rituals featuring wing-flap displays. They will defend and return to their favorite perches. The main species in the North Woods is the American Rubyspot, an unmistakable denizen of larger streams and rivers. However, keep your eyes open along the southern periphery of the North Woods for the Smoky Rubyspot, which has a darker body and dark or smoky wing tips.

River Jewelwing *Calopteryx aequabilis* (male)

♂

C

MAY	JUNE	JULY	AUG	SEPT	OCT

Clean streams, medium-sized or larger, with open canopy. Also small to medium-sized rivers.

Nature Notes:

Male courts female with display of slow alternating wing beats. Male's courtship may include flinging himself onto the water's surface as if to show the female that the current speed in his territory is ideal.

Species name means "equal," perhaps referring to the nearly half black hindwing.

Description: Adults average 2 inches long.

Head, thorax and abdomen bright metallic green, and may appear blue in some light. Male's wings clear at base, banded with black at the tip (↑). Hindwing's black band is larger (1/3 of wing) than forewing band (1/4 of wing). Dark wing bands may be larger on Canadian specimens. Female's wings are light brown to smoky and usually darker at the tip (↑). The white pseudostigma near wing tip of female is conspicuous but slender. Wings of both sexes 3 1/2- to 4-times longer than wide.

Identification Clues: Males are unmistakable; no other North Woods species has a black patch at the wing tip. Female is similar to female Ebony Jewelwing, but River's wings are narrower, usually paler and the white pseudostigma is narrower (less than half as wide as long).

Although the female River Jewelwing's entire wing is often dark, the outer third is usually blacker than the rest.

Life Cycle: Adults emerge primarily in June and often fly into September. Eggs are laid into submerged plant stems. Female may crawl a foot or more below the water's surface to lay eggs and stay submerged for 30 minutes or more. Larvae progress through 12 or 13 molts and are thought to require two or three years to mature.

Ebony Jewelwing *Calopteryx maculata* (male)

MAY	JUNE	JULY	AUG	SEPT	OCT

Small to medium-sized, shaded forest streams. Generally prefers smaller water and more shade than River Jewelwing.

Nature Notes:

After viewing a male's courtship display, a female either says "yes" by opening and closing her wings quickly, or "no" by spreading her wings wide.

Female is blatantly promiscuous, mating up to five times a day and rarely with the same male.

Description: Adults average 1.9 inches long.

Head, thorax and abdomen bright metallic green, may appear blue in some light. Male's wings are broad (3-times as long as wide) and all black (↑). Female's wings are broad, dark brown to smoky and not banded at the tip. White pseudostigma near wing tip of female is conspicuous and broad (↑), nearly half as wide as long.

Identification Clues: Broad, all-black wings of male cannot be mistaken for any other North Woods species. Female is similar to female River Jewelwing, but Ebony's wings are broader, usually darker and the white pseudostigma is wider.

Life Cycle: Adults emerge from late May through July and may fly into September. Eggs are laid into submerged plant stems or logs. Larvae progress through 11 or 12 molts

The broad, all black wings with prominent white pseudostigmas make the female Ebony Jewelwing hard to miss.

and are ready to emerge in one year. Overwinters in one of final two larval instars. Adults live for 16 to 20 days on average, including a teneral period of about 11 days. Females oviposit over a 17-day period during which they may produce nearly 2,000 eggs.

Communal egg laying into a submerged log.

American Rubyspot *Hetaerina americana* (male)

♂

○

MAY	JUNE	JULY	AUG	SEPT	OCT

Gently to rapidly flowing larger streams and rivers.

Nature Notes:

May congregate in densely packed groups. One Ohio odonatist described catching 75 with one sweep of his net!

Flits over shallow riffles where stream banks are well-vegetated. Does not wander far from stream.

Late season species that often flies through September.

Description: Adults average 1.7 inches long. Male's head and thorax are red to reddish brown with thin pale lines along the sutures. Wings are clear with a blood-red patch at the base (↑). Abdomen is metallic bronze to dark brown with pale, narrow rings on middle segments. Female's head and thorax are metallic green or yellow with thin, pale lines along the sutures. Wings are clear or with yellowish to light brown wash, often with amber patch at base (↑). Abdomen shades from metallic green to bronze, with pale, narrow rings on middle segments.

Identification Clues: Blood-red patches at base of male's wings are unmistakable. Lower legs of female are pale; jewelwings have all-black legs.

Life Cycle: Adults emerge in late June and July, and may fly into early October. Eggs are

Females usually have a metallic green thorax but may show more yellow like this one.

laid underwater into plant stems or even partially submerged wood. The larval stage has not been extensively studied. Larvae likely overwinter in the 2nd to 4th instars and are ready to emerge in one year.

Spreadwings
Family Lestidae

The Spreadwings — Genus *Lestes*

The spreadwings differ from all other North Woods damselflies in that they perch with their wings held partially open, at about a 45 degree angle to the body (hence their common name). The only other adult damselfly in our area that perches in this way is the Aurora Damsel, which is easy to separate from the spreadwings by its color pattern and wing venation. A word of caution—don't use the open-winged position to identify tenerals, because they refuse to play by the rules. Some teneral pond damsels hold their wings spread when perched, like spreadwings and newly emerged spreadwings hold their wings together over their backs like pond damsels.

As a group the spreadwings are medium to large in size and are usually found at still-water habitats including temporary ponds. Spreadwings usually are not brightly colored, although the bodies of some are a wonderful iridescent green. Most are gray, brown or black, with various amounts of pruinosity. These drab colors blend in well with the rushes, reeds and sedges of their preferred haunts. Mature males often have bright blue eyes and the tips of the abdomens of most species appear white or grayish-white because of pruinosity. Males tend to become increasingly pruinose with age, often obscuring the underlying colors of the thorax. The wings of spreadwings are narrow, distinctly stalked at the base (called petiolate), not heavily veined and generally clear. The sole exception is the Amber-winged Spreadwing, which has an amber-colored wash on its wings. The wing venation of the group is unique because the position on the wing where the median vein splits sets them apart from pond damsels (see pg. 25).

Many aspects of the spreadwings life cycle are also unique. About two-thirds of our spreadwing species fly late into the season and spend the winter in the egg stage, which no other North Woods genus does. This egg-wintering strategy allows them to live across the entire spectrum of still, freshwater habitats including temporary ponds that dry up by early summer. How do they do that?

All of our damselflies, other than spreadwings, lay their eggs into plant stems near or below the water surface where moisture and increasing temperatures quickly start the egg hatching process. These species all need permanent waters because they spend the winter underwater as larvae. However, female spreadwings of the egg-wintering variety oviposit into the stems of cattails, bulrushes or spikerushes often a foot or more above the water. The eggs immediately take some of the initial developing steps, but before hatching occurs they slip into a state of embryonic diapause. In this state, the drying-resistant eggs spend the winter inside now-dead plant stems where they can withstand temperatures as cold as it gets in the North Woods (with a bit of help from an insulating cover of snow). Then, after the snows melt and water levels rise in the spring, the dead plant stems are wetted, or may fall into the water, providing the moisture needed along with the right temperature and day-length cues to complete the hatching process. Larval life is short for the egg-diapausing species: just two or three months in spring and early summer. This is because the fast-growing larvae need to complete larval development and emerge before the temporary ponds they live in dry up.

The remaining third of our spreadwing species have a more typical damselfly life cycle. They live in permanent ponds, hatch from their eggs in late June, July or August and spend the winter as larvae. Interestingly, females of these larvae-wintering species still oviposit in stems above water even though the strategy now seems unnecessary. With these species, eggs take longer to hatch, and when hatching occurs, the prolarva crawls out of the puncture hole in the plant stem and falls into the water.

Even spreadwing larvae are unique. They are long and slender with long legs. Flip one on its back and you will see an amazingly long labium that is strongly narrowed at its base. No other North Woods damselfly has a labium quite like it. Spreadwing larvae in our region are relatively easy to identify to species by the shape of the labium and the shape and color patterns of the caudal lamellae. Length of the larval stage differs between species that overwinter as larvae versus those that overwinter as eggs. Egg-wintering species only have about ten larval instars and grow really fast. Species that overwinter as larvae have a longer larval life of at least nine months and up to 17 instars.

Spreadwings are usually found along rush-, sedge- and reed-bordered shores of marshes, temporary and permanent ponds and small, sheltered lakes. A few species are infrequently found on slow sections of rivers and streams. The various species have an interesting way of portioning out the habitat they use depending on the permanence of the water body and kinds of predators present. The Swamp Spreadwing and Elegant Spreadwing are able to carve out an existence in permanent ponds with fish predators. The Amber-winged

Spreadwing often dominates in permanent ponds that lack fish. These three species overwinter as larvae. Our other species seem to do best in temporary ponds that lack fish, where the top predators are usually dragonfly larvae. However, the Northern Spreadwing, Sweetflag Spreadwing and Spotted Spreadwing are sometimes found in permanent ponds and streams. The Emerald Spreadwing does best in temporary pools that lack both fish and dragonfly predators. Even though these vernal pools dry out by early summer, Emerald Spreadwing larvae have such explosively fast growth rates that they can complete larval development and emerge before then. Wherever they live, adult spreadwings flit from stem to stem along the shore in short flights, feeding primarily on small flies that have emerged from the same areas. The name *Lestes* means "robber," probably referring to the predatory habits of this genus.

Approximately 160 species of Lestidae are known worldwide, of which about 18 are found in North America. Nine species, all in the genus *Lestes*, are found in the North Woods, while a tenth, the Southern Spreadwing (*Lestes disjunctus australis*), may occur at the southern periphery. All males can be identified in the hand by the definitive shapes of their terminal appendages (claspers). Some species (both sexes) can be identified in the field because of their unique body shape, body coloration, wing coloration or elongate ovipositor. However, females of a few species can only be identified under a microscope, primarily by subtle differences in the lengths of some abdominal segments and the shape of the basal plate of the ovipositor. The Southern Spreadwing presents a bit of a thorny issue for us here in the North Woods for a couple of reasons. First, it's unclear if it is a distinct species or a subspecies of the Northern Spreadwing. Second, the males are so similar to the Sweetflag Spreadwing that they can only be differentiated under a microscope and even then, specialists can have trouble telling them apart. The result is that the range of the Southern Spreadwing is not well known. Odonatists who study damselflies in the North Woods believe the Southern Spreadwing rarely occurs this far north, but we don't really know for sure.

Top view of male's claspers

Side view of female's abdomen tip

Amber-winged Spreadwing
Lestes eurinus

Note rounded margin of basal plate

Elegant Spreadwing
L. inaequalis

Note angled margin of basal plate

Swamp Spreadwing
L. vigilax

Emerald Spreadwing
L. dryas

Slender Spreadwing
L. rectangularis

Lyre-tipped Spreadwing
L. unguiculatus

Sweetflag Spreadwing
L. forcipatus

Northern Spreadwing
L. disjunctus

Spotted Spreadwing
L. congener

Amber-winged Spreadwing *Lestes eurinus* (male)

MAY	JUNE	JULY	AUG	SEPT	OCT

Small lakes and ponds, usually permanent and usually lacking fish.

Nature Notes:

One of our largest spreadwings and one of the earliest to appear.

Species name refers to the east wind; no one seems to know how this applies to the insect.

Description: Adults average 2 inches long.

Large and stout-bodied. Head, thorax and abdomen of male metallic green above, abruptly turning to pale yellow below with a pair of dark vertical bands. The last two abdominal segments are grayish-white pruinose. Pruinosity on thorax develops with age obscuring much of the underlying color pattern. Wings entirely covered with an amber wash (↑). Female is similar and also shows the two dark bands on lower thorax (↑).

Identification Clues: Honey-colored wings and large size readily separate this species from all other spreadwings. Shapes and relative sizes of terminal appendages of male are diagnostic, with cerci more than twice as long as paraprocts (pg. 37). Identify females by large size and rounded margin of basal plate of ovipositor (pg. 37).

The heavy-bodied female Amber-winged Spreadwing is one of the most robust damselflies in the North Woods.

Life Cycle: Adults emerge in June and July and may fly through August. After emerging, females may require up to a month to mature. American Bur-Reed (*Sparganium americanum*) is the favored plant for egg laying. Eggs are laid into stems above water and take about 45 days to develop. Upon hatching, the prolarva emerges from the cut in the stem, falls into the water and molts into the second instar within three minutes. The larval period spans about nine months and includes 13 to 17 instars. Overwintering occurs during one of the last three larval instars.

Elegant Spreadwing *Lestes inaequalis* (male)

♂

MAY	JUNE	JULY	AUG	SEPT	OCT

Wide variety of permanent ponds, small lakes, lagoons and slow streams.

Nature Notes:

Elegant is a great name for this large, handsome and slender spreadwing.

Species name means "unequal", referring to the paraprocts of the male being distinctly longer than the cerci (pg. 37).

Description: Adults average 2.1 inches long.

Large and slender bodied. Thorax and abdomen of male is bright green above and pale yellow below (↑). Last two abdominal segments are grayish-white pruinose. Pruinosity on thorax develops less fully than on other spreadwings. Wings clear. Female is similar to male overall, but duller. Female may not always be distinguishable from Swamp Spreadwing female except under a microscope.

Identification Clues: Terminal appendages of male are unmistakable with paraprocts longer than cerci (pg. 37). Distinguish females from Amber-winged Spreadwing by Elegant's clear wings, lack of vertical dark bands on side of thorax and angular basal plate of ovipositor. Distinguish females from Swamp Spreadwing by Elegant's pale yellow on lower legs (tibiae) (↑) and back of head.

The female Elegant Spreadwing is very similar to the male but not quite as bright.

Life Cycle: Adults emerge in June and July and may fly into August. Life history of this species has not been thoroughly studied. Eggs are laid into emergent plant stems above water. Upon hatching, the prolarva emerges from the cut in the stem, falls into the water and quickly molts into the second instar. Overwintering likely occurs during one of the last three larval instars.

Swamp Spreadwing *Lestes vigilax* (male)

MAY	JUNE	JULY	AUG	SEPT	OCT

Wide variety of permanent waters including marshy and bog-bordered ponds, small acidic lakes and slow streams.

Nature Notes:

Species name means "watchful." Only Hermann Hagen, who named this species in 1862, knew why it is more watchful than others.

Often abundant where it occurs.

Mainly found during the second half of summer.

Description: Adults average 2 inches long.

Large and slender bodied. Thorax and abdomen of male is metallic green above and pale yellow turning with age to whitish pruinose below (↑). Thin brown shoulder stripes (↑) often visible. Last two abdominal segments are grayish-white pruinose. Wings clear. Female is similar to male overall, but duller. Female may not always be distinguishable from female Elegant Spreadwing except under a microscope.

Identification Clues: Terminal appendages of male are unmistakable with paraprocts long, thin and straight (pg. 37). Distinguish females from Amber-winged by Swamp's clear wings, lack of vertical dark bands on side of thorax and angular basal plate of ovipositor. Distinguish females from Elegant Spreadwing by dark lower legs (↑) and dark back of head.

Like many spreadwings, the female Swamp Spreadwing closely resembles the male.

Life Cycle: Adults emerge in June and July and may fly into September. Surprisingly, little life history information is available about this widespread and fairly common species. Eggs are laid into emergent plant stems above water. Upon hatching, the prolarva emerges from the cut in the stem, falls into the water and quickly molts into the second instar. The larval period spans at least nine months. Overwintering occurs during one of the middle larval instars.

Emerald Spreadwing *Lestes dryas* (male)

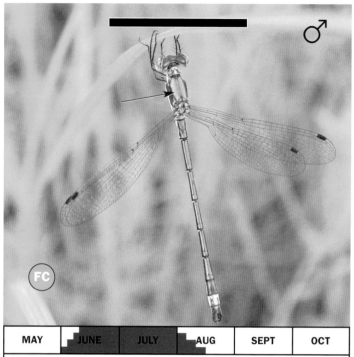

MAY	JUNE	JULY	AUG	SEPT	OCT

Small woodland ponds and pools that dry up by summer (a.k.a. vernal pools); occasionally permanent ponds.

Nature Notes:

Species name refers to a mythical Greek wood nymph, perhaps indicating its preference for shaded, forest pools.

Thrives in shallow, temporary, woodland pools that lack fish and insect predators.

Description: Adults average 1.5 inches long.

One of the smaller spreadwings and the stockiest. Thorax and abdomen of male is bright metallic green above (↑) and pale yellow turning whitish pruinose below (↑). Last two abdominal segments are grayish-white pruinose. Wings clear. Female is also metallic green (↑), but with thin, pale shoulder stripes and a thicker abdomen. Female has a long ovipositor that extends beyond tip of abdomen (↑) (like Sweetflag Spreadwing female).

Identification Clues: Boot-shaped paraprocts of male are diagnostic (pg. 37). Brighter green and heavier bodied than other spreadwings. Female Sweetflag Spreadwing has

Female Emerald Spreadwing shows the same bright green top of thorax and abdomen as the male, but note her very long ovipositor that extends beyond the tip of the abdomen.

an even longer ovipositor and the top of her thorax is dark, not bright green.

Life Cycle: Adults emerge in June and early July. Flight period usually ends by early August. Eggs are laid into emergent plant stems, often bulrushes, above water. Eggs are large, hence the need for the female's large ovipositor. Eggs hatch in early spring after pools fill with spring run-off. Upon hatching, the prolarva emerges from the cut in the stem and quickly molts into the second instar. The larvae develop extraordinarily quickly through ten instars in just a few months. Overwinters as eggs in late stages of embryonic development where they can withstand air temperatures lower than minus 4 degrees F. May overwinter as larvae in milder climates.

Older males become increasingly whitish pruinose on the lower thorax.

Slender Spreadwing *Lestes rectangularis* (male)

♂

| MAY | JUNE | JULY | AUG | SEPT | OCT |

Shallow and partially shaded still-water habitats: temporary and permanent ponds, marshes and backwaters of slow streams.

Nature Notes:

Male is readily identified at a glance by his peculiarly long and thin abdomen.

Female lays eggs alone, not with a male clinging to her.

Description: Adults average 1.8 inches long.

A long, slender spreadwing. Thorax and abdomen of male dark above with pale yellow sides. Thorax has wide, bluish shoulder stripes that are often partly gray. Lacks pruinosity at tip of abdomen. Wings clear with pale vein at outer tip (↑). Female is similar to the male but her abdomen is shorter. Female ovipositor short, not extending beyond tip of abdomen.

Identification Clues: Male is easily identified by an abdomen that is twice as long as his wings (↑) and the downturned tips of his paraprocts seen in profile (↑) (see opposite page). Female Northern Spreadwing, Slender Spreadwing and Lyre-tipped Spreadwing are very similar. Positive identification of females of these species is based on subtle differences in lengths of some abdominal segments seen under a microscope.

Female Slender Spreadwing also has a long slender abdomen and her pale shoulder stripe often shows various amounts of gray.

Life Cycle: Adults emerge from mid June through July and often fly well into September. Eggs are laid into a variety of plant stems, including bulrushes and cat-tails, above water level. Eggs hatch in spring, at which time the prolarva emerges from the cut in the stem and quickly molts into the second instar. Larval development takes about twelve weeks and maturation requires about three weeks after emergence. Overwinters as eggs in various stages of development.

The slender long abdomen is easy to see, even at a distance.

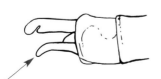

The distinctive profile of the male Slender Spreadwing's claspers.

Note the gray area on the pale shoulder stripe of this immature male.

Lyre-tipped Spreadwing *Lestes unguiculatus* (male)

♂

| MAY | JUNE | JULY | AUG | SEPT | OCT |

Small, sunny ponds that are often temporary in at least some years.

Nature Notes:

Six or more pairs in tandem have been seen laying eggs in a single bulrush stem.

Species name means "small-clawed," perhaps referring to the clawed shape of the male's paraprocts. "Lyre-tipped" also refers to these distinctly shaped structures (see middle photo on opposite page).

Description: Adults average 1.5 inches long.

Small for a spreadwing. Thorax of male is bronze with pale green shoulder stripes (↑), turning pale yellow to whitish below. Thorax becomes increasingly pruinose with age. Abdomen metallic green, with last two segments grayish-white pruinose and segment 8 partially pruinose (↑). Wings clear. Female's thorax is similar to male's but her abdomen is dark with greenish reflections on top and thicker. Rear of female's head often pale. Female's ovipositor is short, not extending beyond the tip of her abdomen.

Identification Clues: Male's S-shaped paraprocts (↑) with divergent tips are diagnostic (pg. 37). Female Northern Spreadwing and Slender Spreadwing are very similar to Lyre-tipped, but they have a dark rear of head. Separation of females of these species in this

Note the stocky appearance and green reflections on top of the abdomen of this female Lyre-tipped Spreadwing.

way is tentative. Positive identification is based on subtle differences in lengths of some abdominal segments seen under a microscope.

Life Cycle: Adults emerge from mid June through early July and fly into September. Eggs are laid into emergent plant stems, often bulrushes, from two inches to two feet above water level. Eggs hatch in spring when water temperatures reach about 50 degrees F. Upon hatching, the prolarva emerges from the cut

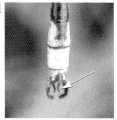

The male's S-shaped paraprocts form the lyre in Lyre-tipped.

in the stem, drops into the water and quickly molts into the second instar. Larval development takes about 60 days and maturation requires 16 to 18 days after emergence. Overwinters as eggs that can withstand air temperatures to about minus 4 degrees F. Snow cover is essential to protect eggs from very cold temperatures.

Note the male's diagnostic pale green shoulder stripes.

Sweetflag Spreadwing *Lestes forcipatus* (male)

MAY	JUNE	JULY	AUG	SEPT	OCT

Well-vegetated or boggy ponds, pools and marshes, often temporary and lacking fish; occasionally in slow streams.

Nature Notes:

Species name means "bearing forceps," perhaps alluding to the shape of the male's cerci.

Emerges earlier in season than the similar Northern Spreadwing.

Eggs are laid almost exclusively into the stems of Sweet Flag (*Acorus calamus*).

Description: Adults average 1.6 inches long. A mid-sized, dark spreadwing. Thorax and abdomen of male dark above with pale yellow or grayish-white sides. Lower side of thorax may have a black spot (↑). Thorax has pale or dark shoulder stripes. Dark coloration on thorax becomes more extensive with age and is eventually obscured by pruinosity. Last two abdominal segments are grayish-white pruinose. Wings clear. Female similar to male but sides of her thorax are often light tan and her abdomen thicker. Rear of female's head can be dark or pale. Female's ovipositor is long, extending beyond the tip of her abdomen (↑).

Identification Clues: Separate male from male Northern Spreadwing by Sweetflag's two unequal teeth on cerci, end tooth is smaller and blunter than basal tooth; also, teeth are further apart (pg. 37). See cautions in spread-

The female Sweetflag Spreadwing is easy to spot because of her long ovipositor.

wing introduction (pg. 36) about the very similar male Southern Spreadwing. Female is unmistakable; only the female Emerald Spreadwing has an ovipositor nearly as long, but she has bright metallic green (not dark) on top of her thorax and abdomen.

Life Cycle: Adults emerge in June and July and fly into September. Eggs are laid into Sweet Flag (*Acorus calamus*) stems above water level. Eggs hatch in early spring, at which time the prolarva emerges from the cut in the stem and quickly molts into the second instar. Larval development through about ten instars takes less than two months. Overwinters as eggs that can withstand air temperatures to about minus 4 degrees F.

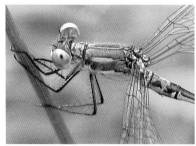

Note the bright blue eyes that are typical of most male spreadwings.

Northern Spreadwing *Lestes disjunctus* (male)

MAY	JUNE	JULY	AUG	SEPT	OCT

Still-water habitats. Marshy or boggy ponds that may be permanent or temporary. Also bogs, fens and slow streams.

Nature Notes:

Most abundant and widespread spreadwing in the North Woods. It was formerly called the Common Spreadwing.

Two males may struggle while attempting to form a tandem pair with the same female.

Description: Adults average 1.5 inches long. A small, dark spreadwing. Thorax and abdomen of male is dark above with pale yellow or gray sides. Thorax has pale greenish-blue shoulder stripes (↑). Dark color on thorax becomes more extensive with age and is eventually obscured by pruinosity. Last two segments of abdomen are grayish-white pruinose. Wings clear. Female is similar to male but sides of her thorax are yellow to light tan and her abdomen is thicker. Rear of female's head is dark. Female ovipositor is short, not extending beyond tip of abdomen (↑).

Identification Clues: Two equal-sized "teeth" on each cercus of male can be seen with a hand lens (pg. 37). Female Northern Spreadwing, Slender Spreadwing and Lyre-tipped Spreadwing are very similar. Positive identification of females of these species is

♀

Separating female Northern Spreadwings from female Lyre-tipped and Slender Spreadwings is best left to experts with a microscope.

based on subtle differences in lengths of some abdominal segments seen under a microscope. See cautions in spreadwing introduction (pg. 36) about the closely related Southern Spreadwing.

Life Cycle: Adults have a long flight period, emerging in late June and July and often flying into September. Eggs are usually laid into the green stems of bulrushes, above water level. Eggs hatch in spring when water temperatures reach about 50 degrees F. Upon hatching, the prolarva emerges from the cut in the stem and quickly molts into the second instar. Larval development through ten instars takes about 60 days and maturation requires 16 to 18 days after emergence. Overwinters as eggs that can withstand air temperatures to about minus 4 degrees F. Snow cover is essential to protect eggs from very cold temperatures.

Spotted Spreadwing *Lestes congener* (male)

MAY	JUNE	JULY	AUG	SEPT	OCT

Permanent and temporary still-water habitats: marshy and bog-bordered ponds, swamps, marshes and slow streams.

Nature Notes:

Our latest damselfly, often seen into mid October.

Common and widespread in the North Woods.

Species name means "of the same kind," possibly to include them with others of the same genus.

Description: Adults average 1.4 inches long. A small, dark and stocky spreadwing. Thorax and abdomen of male is dark above with pale whitish gray sides and a pair of dark spots on lower edge of thorax (↑). Thorax has very thin, pale shoulder stripes. Pruinosity on the thorax becomes more extensive with age. Last two segments of abdomen are grayish-white pruinose. Wings clear. Female is similar to male but with a thicker abdomen. Female ovipositor is short, not extending beyond tip of abdomen.

Identification Clues: Both sexes are easy to identify by the presence of a pair of dark spots on the lower edge of the thorax.

Life Cycle: Adults begin to emerge in July and peak abundance is reached in September. Some fly well into October. Eggs are laid into dry bulrush stems above water level. Eggs hatch in late spring, at which time the prolar-

Both the male and female Spotted Spreadwings show a distinctive pair of spots along the lower edge of the thorax. The Sweetflag Spreadwing may have a single spot here.

va emerges from the cut in the stem and quickly molts into the second instar. Larval development through ten instars takes about 50 days. Newly emerged adults require three weeks to mature. Overwinters as eggs but in an earlier state of embryonic development than other spreadwings. Eggs survive air temperatures at least as low as minus 18 degrees F.

The spots along the lower edge of the thorax of this male give this species its common name.

Pond Damsels
Family Coenagrionidae

The pond damsels comprise a huge family of mostly small, clear-winged species that delightfully display nearly all the colors of the rainbow. This family includes our smallest damselflies, some of which barely reach an inch long, and many of our most common species. Aspects of wing venation are the unifying features that set them apart from other families (see Family Key on pg. 25). Their stigmas are short, less than twice as long as wide. The male's terminal appendages are shorter than in other families, and the legs are quite short as well. Females often come in two color schemes: a male-like color pattern (homeochromatic) and a color pattern different than the male (heterochromatic).

Pond damsels inhabit the full spectrum of aquatic breeding habitats in the North Woods: lakes, ponds, marshes, swamps, bogs, fens, rivers, streams and spring seeps. Some species are habitat generalists that can be found at almost any aquatic site whereas others are closely tied to specific types of habitat (specialists). Adults can often be found near breeding sites around clearings, meadows, along roadways and railroad grades. They fly from May through September in the North Woods, although most species have a short flight period lasting only four to six weeks.

Worldwide there are over 1,100 described species of pond damsels, with about 105 species in North America north of Mexico. This is easily the largest damselfly family in the North Woods, with 27 resident species and six species that may stray into the area.

Dancers — Genus *Argia*

The Dancers are a colorful group of damselflies of medium build and moderate to large size. Males are predominantly blue or purple and females are olive or brown. They may lose their bright colors when they get cold, but regain them when they warm up. They are known for their bouncy flight (hence the common name) and their tendency to alight on bare, sunny places such as roads, paths and shoreline rocks. Dancers are alert, tend not to rest long in one spot and may be hard to approach. North Woods species are usually found along flowing waters or the wave-beaten shores of large lakes. Males arrive at breeding sites before females. They fly aggressively at other males, but without physical contact and with little clear defense of territories. Females deposit eggs into wet wood or in mats of floating plant material, often at communal sites. Females usually oviposit in tandem, with males alertly guarding in the "sentinel" position, but they may also be unattended. Larvae live in gently moving water either under rocks in rapids or in mud and detritus in quieter areas. The larvae are easy to recognize with their short, stocky bodies and wide caudal lamellae. The most likely meaning for the name *Argia* is "lazy," but no one seems to known how this applies to the group. *Argia* may have been intended to mean "bright," from the Greek *argos*, referring to the coloration of the males.

This is a Neotropical genus of about 120 species, most living in Central and South America. Currently, 32 species are recognized in North America, with four occurring in the North Woods. Dancers are easily separated from all other pond damsels by the long spurs on their lower legs (tibiae). These spurs are twice as long as the spaces between them. The highly stalked shape of the wings is also unique to the dancers. The male's terminal appendages have cerci shorter than their paraprocts. Females lack a vulvar spine on abdominal segment 8. Our males are easily identified in the field or in the hand by their colors and patterns. Females can usually be identified in the hand.

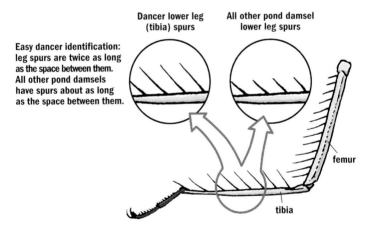

Dancer lower leg (tibia) spurs

All other pond damsel lower leg spurs

Easy dancer identification: leg spurs are twice as long as the space between them. All other pond damsels have spurs about as long as the space between them.

femur

tibia

Red Damsels — Genus *Amphiagrion* (Text on page 69)

Aurora Damsel — Genus *Chromagrion* (Text on page 71)

Eurasian Bluets — Genus *Coenagrion* (Text on page 72)

American Bluets — Genus *Enallagma* (Text on page 78)

Forktails — Genus *Ischnura* (Text on page 108)

Sprites — Genus *Nehalennia* (Text on page 116)

Abdomen tip side views of male Pond Damsels

Violet Dancer

Powdered Dancer

Blue-fronted Dancer

Blue-tipped Dancer

Eastern Red Damsel

Aurora Damsel

Taiga Bluet

Subarctic Bluet

Orange Bluet

Vesper Bluet

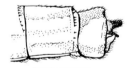

Rainbow Bluet

Azure Bluet

Stream Bluet

Skimming Bluet

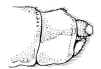

Tule Bluet

Familiar Bluet

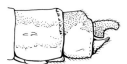

River Bluet

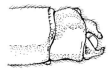

Alkali Bluet

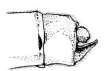

Boreal Bluet

Northern Bluet

Marsh Bluet

Hagen's Bluet

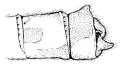

Eastern Forktail

Fragile Forktail

Citrine Forktail

Sedge Sprite

Sphagnum Sprite

Violet Dancer *Argia fumipennis violacea* (male)

MAY	JUNE	JULY	AUG	SEPT	OCT

Clear, gentle streams and stream backwaters. Also some lakes.

Nature Notes:

Male is strikingly attractive—our only mostly purple damselfly.

Male assumes "sentinel" position while female oviposits (see lower photo on opposite page).

Flies most actively in morning and during midday.

Description: Adults average 1.2 inches long.

A small, easily identified dancer. Thorax and abdomen of male is mostly violet, with a black, forked shoulder stripe (↑) on each side and narrow black rings on most abdominal segments. Younger male is violet-blue (see inset photo above). Tops of segments 8, 9 and 10 are powder blue. Female is mostly brown with thin, forked shoulder stripes and thin, longitudinal black stripes (↑) on most abdominal segments. Wings of both sexes clear. Two subspecies that occur further south and east have smoky or very dark wings.

Identification Clues: Violet color and forked shoulder stripes of male are unmistakable. Female separable from female Blue-tipped Dancer by her thinner forked shoulder stripe and lighter-colored abdomen on top. Other female dancers lack a forked shoulder stripe.

With her thin, dark shoulder stripes, the female Violet Dancer is easy to recognize.

Life Cycle: Adults have a long flight period, beginning to emerge in mid June and flying late into September. Pair oviposits in tandem on wet logs and other plant materials but does not descend below water's surface. Larvae lurk on plant stems and on other bottom debris. The larval stage is not well known. Overwinters as a larva, probably in one of the last larval instars.

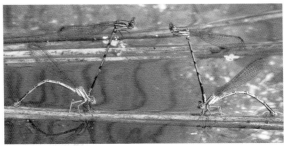

Two pairs of Violet Dancers ovipositing (laying eggs) with males contact-guarding in the sentinel position.

Powdered Dancer *Argia moesta* (male)

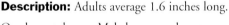

MAY	JUNE	JULY	AUG	SEPT	OCT

Rock-margined streams, rivers and lakes.

Nature Notes:

Our only whitish damselfly due to the male's extensive pruinosity.

Our largest pond damsel.

Pairs may spend an hour or more underwater while laying eggs!

Description: Adults average 1.6 inches long.

Our largest dancer. Male becomes almost completely whitish (↑) when mature as pruinosity covers most of his body. Immature males are tan to dark brown, turning darker with age before becoming pruinose. Wide, dark shoulder stripes of male become obscured by pruinosity. Female's thorax is brown or blue with hairline dark shoulder stripes (↑). Her abdomen with pale, wide top stripe and narrow dark side stripes, often noticeably pale at tip. Wings of both sexes clear.

Identification Clues: Extensive whitish pruinosity of male is unique. Our only dancer with two cells below the stigma of the wing, separated in the middle by a crossvein (both sexes). Female very similar to female Blue-fronted Dancer.

This blue-form female was photographed on a rock—a very characteristic perch for this species.

Life Cycle: Adults have a long flight period, beginning to emerge in early June and flying into September. Tenerals require two weeks after emergence to mature. Pairing occurs throughout the summer months. Pair descends, usually in tandem, sometimes deep underwater to oviposit in wet wood or algae-covered rocks and may remain submerged for an hour or more! Larvae lurk under stones and other bottom debris. The larval stage is not well known. Overwinters as a larva, probably in one of the last larval instars. Emergence-perches are usually rocks or logs well above water.

Older Powdered Dancer males turn nearly white with age.

Blue-fronted Dancer *Argia apicalis* (male)

MAY	JUNE	JULY	AUG	SEPT	OCT

Smaller rivers and streams with gentle current; occasionally lakes and ponds.

Nature Notes:

Flies with a "dancing" movement over streamside vegetation.

Male's bright blue thorax is easily seen when he is perched on bare ground.

Description: Adults average 1.5 inches long. A brightly colored and slender species. Adult males show bright blue on the thorax (↑) and on top of last three abdominal segments while the rest of abdomen is dark. Dark shoulder stripes are hairline thin. Female is either brown or blue like the male. Her abdomen is dark on top with a narrow pale stripe on some segments and a dark side stripe on segment 9 (↑). Wings of both sexes clear.

Identification Clues: Bright blue thorax of male with only a hairline shoulder stripe is unmistakable. Female is very similar to female Powdered Dancer, both of which have very thin shoulder stripes. Female Blue-fronted has only one cell in wing directly below the stigma whereas female Powdered Dancer usually has two cells there (with a crossvein below the middle of the stigma).

Brown-form female Blue-fronted Dancers blend well with the rocky or sandy surfaces they normally land on.

Life Cycle: Adults have a long flight period, beginning to emerge in mid June and flying into September. Individual adults live about a month at most. Females may congregate to oviposit below the water's surface into well-decayed logs. Larvae evidently lurk on under-water plants and among bottom detritus. The larval stage is poorly known. Overwinters as a larva, likely in one of the last larval instars.

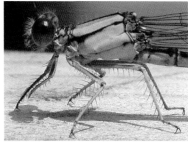

This blue-form female's thorax is colored like the male's.

Blue-tipped Dancer *Argia tibialis* (male)

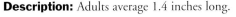

MAY	JUNE	JULY	AUG	SEPT	OCT

Small to mid-sized streams, slow or fast flowing, with banks having some shade. Occasionally sloughs and ponds.

Nature Notes:

Prefers shade and is more likely to perch in vegetation than our other dancers.

Look for the Blue-tipped in southerly areas of the North Woods.

Description: Adults average 1.4 inches long.

A smallish, dark dancer. Male is mostly dark, with pale shoulder stripes that are wide and purplish (↑) or brown. Dark shoulder stripes are wide and black. Top of segments 9 and 10 are powder blue. Female's thorax is blue or brown with a wide, dark shoulder stripe forked at top forming a small pale blue triangle (↑). Female's abdomen is dark like male's, but with segment 10 light brown (↑). Wings clear.

Identification Clues: Male is our only dancer with a dark thorax and pale blue abdomen tip. Female is our only dancer with wide, dark shoulder stripe that is forked at the top forming a pale blue triangle.

Life Cycle: Adults have a long flight period, beginning to emerge by mid June and flying through August. Female oviposits in wet wood and other plant material. Reproduction and

Female Blue-tipped Dancer may show brown on the thorax or blue, like this one.

early life stages are not well known. Larvae
lurk under stones and other bottom debris.
Overwinters as a larva, likely in one of the last
larval instars.

Eastern Red Damsel *Amphiagrion saucium* (male)

MAY	JUNE	JULY	AUG	SEPT	OCT

Gently flowing spring-fed streams, spring ponds or spring upwellings. Also at margins of bogs, ponds or ditches.

Nature Notes:

Its need for spring upwellings means it may disappear from areas where the water table has been lowered.

Areas of preferred habitat are often small, but capable of producing many individuals.

Flies close to the ground in vegetation, avoiding open water.

Description: Adults average one inch long.

Small, stocky, two-tone species. Male is mostly red (↑) with dark areas (↑) that increase in size with age on top of the thorax and on the last three or four abdominal segments. Female is similar but duller, without the dark area on top of thorax. Her thorax and abdomen are mostly brownish orange with reddish highlights on the abdomen (↑). Head and eyes are reddish brown without eyespots. Wings clear. Male has prominent, hairy "bump" on underside of thorax. Female has strong vulvar spine.

Identification Clues: Our only two-tone, red-and-dark damselfly that lacks eyespots. Downward sloping cerci of the male (seen in the hand) are diagnostic (pg. 58). Look for the lack of eyespots and no black areas on the female; other female pond damsels that show orange have eyespots and black areas on the thorax.

The female Eastern Red Damsel's completely reddish-orange body with no black areas or eyespots separates her from all other species. Note the mites on the underside of her thorax.

Life Cycle: Adults have a short flight period, emerging in late May or June and flying though July. Mating, egg-laying and larval life have not been studied. Probably overwinters in one of the last few larval instars.

Red Damsels
Genus *Amphiagrion*

This beautiful little genus contains only two species, the only red damselflies in the North Woods. Interestingly, populations in the Midwest are intermediate between Eastern and Western Red Damsels. Specimens in the North Woods are most like the eastern species, and will be referred to as such until new study results shed further light on the situation. Larvae of this species and the Aurora Damsel are distinctive in having sharply angled rear corners of the head. Genus name means "both Agrion (a word for damselfly)," probably referring to the two species in the genus.

Aurora Damsel *Chromagrion conditum* (male)

MAY	JUNE	JULY	AUG	SEPT	OCT

Shady, spring-fed streams, especially pools and slow backwaters; sometimes clean ponds.

Nature Notes:

Perched males hold their wing partially outspread like spreadwings, though not quite as widely apart.

North Woods populations are usually quite local.

Adults stay close to shelter and spend little time on the wing.

Description: Adults average 1.4 inches long.

A large and slender, strikingly colored pond damsel. Male's thorax is distinctive; black above with wavy edges (↑), blue sides and a unique yellow blotch on the lower side. Abdomen is mostly black with thin, blue rings on middle segments and blue patches on top near the tip. Female is similar to male, including black on top with wavy edging and a yellow side blotch (↑) that may be pale. Her thorax may be blue but is usually pale brown or gray where his is blue. Wings clear. No eyespots.

Identification Clues: The only North Woods damselfly with a thorax having a large black area with wavy edges on top, no shoulder stripes and a yellow side blotch. Long, curved shape of male's cerci is unmistakable (pg. 58). All American and Eurasian bluets in North Woods have obvious eyespots.

You can just see the characteristic yellow blotch on the lower thorax of this female Aurora Damsel.

Life Cycle: Adults emerge in June and fly into August. Emergence perches are plant stems a few inches above water and often further from shore than other species. The male seizes the female while perched and quickly forms tandem position. Egg-laying occurs while in tandem, with the male guarding in the sentinel position. Female inserts eggs in or on plant stems just below water's surface. Hatching occurs about three weeks later. Overwinters in late larval instars.

Aurora Damsel
Genus *Chromagrion*

The Aurora Damsel is the only species in its genus, and occurs only in eastern North America. It is unlike other members of the pond damsel family in the way it holds its wings, in aspects of wing venation and in the long terminal appendages of the males. Larvae have distinctively angled rear corners of the head, as do the red damsels. Genus name means "colored Agrion (a word for damselfly)," referring to the distinctive blue and yellow hues on the thorax.

Eurasian Bluets
Genus *Coenagrion*

The Eurasian bluets are a northern group of small to medium-sized damselflies that I find to be exceptionally beautiful. Males of the Taiga Bluet are especially compelling, with shades of blue and green on their thorax and abdomen that are hard to adequately describe. Males of most species are primarily blue and black and can easily be mistaken for male American bluets (genus *Enallagma*) or even forktails (genus *Ischnura*). Females are marked similar to the males and come in two basic color patterns: male-like hues (homeochromatic) and duller, greenish or brownish hues (heterochromatic). Adults tend to fly low and perch often among vegetation. North Woods species are usually found along the edges of ponds, marshes and bogs. Males arrive at breeding sites before females. They are rarely aggressive with other damselflies and do not defend territories. Females oviposit in tandem on emergent or floating vegetation with males alertly guarding in the "sentinel" position.

Larvae live in still, often shallow waters where they crawl about on submerged vegetation hunting their prey. The larvae are small and brown or greenish and are very similar to larvae of American bluets, from which they are difficult to separate. North American species generally complete their life cycle in one year, but in the Far North development is slower, possibly taking as long as three or four years. This genus is better able to tolerate colder climates than any other group. A fascinating study found that the larvae of the Taiga Bluet and the Prairie Bluet overwintered embedded in five to eight inches of ice! They were often found completely encased in an upside-down position as though trapped while walking about on the undersurface of the ice, and when the ice melted they resumed activity. The ability to overwinter in this way allows them to survive in shallow northern ponds that freeze to the bottom in winter and protects them from predators.

This is a circumpolar boreal group that occurs around the world, with most species occurring in Europe and Asia. Only three species are found in North America, two of which are found in the North Woods and the third is possible here as well. The Taiga Bluet is fairly widespread and common, though rarely abundant at any site. The Subarctic Bluet is one of our rarest damselflies. Keep your eyes open also for the Prairie Bluet, which may occur along the western edge of the North Woods. Eurasian bluet males differ from male American bluets by subtle differences in the shape of their reproductive organs. Females are easily separated in the hand from American bluets by their lack of a vulvar spine on abdominal segment 8 (all American bluet females have it). Our males are easily identified to species in the field by their colors and patterns. The shapes of their terminal appendages are diagnostic as well. Females can be trickier to separate but can usually be identified in the hand.

Taiga Bluet *Coenagrion resolutum* (male)

MAY	JUNE	JULY	AUG	SEPT	OCT

Wide variety of still waters from marshy ponds and grassy ditches to bogs, fens and slow streams.

Nature Notes:

Ranges above the Arctic Circle in Canada—all the way to the Arctic Ocean!

Larvae overwinter embedded in ice but do not freeze solid!

Species name means "resolute," underscoring the fortitude they possess to eke out an existence in inhospitable northern climates.

Description: Adults average 1.2 inches long.

Attractive combination of blue, green and black. Male's thorax is blue with a wide black top stripe and thinner black shoulder stripes. Sides of thorax blue, shading to green below (↑). Abdomen is blue and black; segment 2 with a U-shaped dorsal black mark (↑). Segments 6 and 7 mostly black, 8 and 9 entirely blue. Female is similar, but with top of her abdomen almost entirely black. Pale areas are either blue like male or yellowish green. Wings clear.

Identification Clues: Identify males by blue-green color on side of thorax and U-shaped black mark on top of segment 2. Shape of male terminal appendages is diagnostic (pg. 58). In females, look for blue-green sides on thorax (↑) and the lack of a vulvar spine.

The female Taiga Bluet resembles several female American bluets but lacks a vulvar spine on abdomen segment 9.

Life Cycle: Adults emerge from late May to late June when water temperature exceed 54 degrees F. Sexual maturation takes about one week. Pairing and egg laying commence in early June and adults may fly late into July. Mating occurs at the site of maturation, about 100 yards away from the pond, without courtship or territorial behavior. Oviposition is always in tandem and occurs below the surface into rushes, cattails, pondweed and other standing or floating aquatic plants. Eggs hatch within three weeks. Larval growth is relatively slow compared to fast growers like larval spreadwings, extending for a period of ten to 22 months. Overwinters in larval diapause and embedded in ice in one of the last three instars, surviving temperatures as low as 23 degrees F.

Subarctic Bluet *Coenagrion interrogatum* (male)

♂

R

MAY	JUNE	JULY	AUG	SEPT	OCT

Cold swamps and open bogs, especially quaking sphagnum moss margins around bog ponds.

Nature Notes:

One of the rarest damselflies in the North Woods.

The southern limit of its distribution is further north than any other damselfly.

Found at Churchill on Hudson Bay and northwest to the Yukon Territories.

Description: Adults average 1.2 inches long.

Both sexes are a study in blue and black. The pale shoulder stripes on the thorax are wide and bordered and divided with back, which forms a pale blue square and rectangle (↑) on the shoulder. The abdomen is blue and black, with the patterns on segment 2 unlike any other species. Pale eyespots are prominent on the otherwise dark head. Wings clear.

Identification Clues: Males have unique dark markings including the pale shoulder stripe feature described above and the underside of the thorax, which is extensively black including a Y-shaped figure. The shape of the male's terminal appendages is diagnostic (pg. 58). The female's thorax undersides are heavily marked with black and she shows long black streaks on the sides of her abdomen (↑).

The female Subarctic Bluet is extensively marked with black on her lower thorax and sides of her abdomen.

Life Cycle: Flight season is early and relatively short, with emergence beginning in mid May to early June. Adults lay eggs throughout June and perhaps into July. Sexual maturation takes about one week. Oviposition has not been described and the early larval stages are poorly known. Likely overwinters in one of the last three larval instars.

American Bluets
Genus *Enallagma*

The American bluets are a large genus of small to mid-sized species that are abundant in the North Woods around a wide variety of still-water habitats. They are commonly called "bluets" because the males of most species are primarily blue with contrasting black markings that consist of distinct stripes on the thorax and bands on the abdomen. While glancing through the field notebook of an Ontario friend a few years ago I saw reference to "lots of BBBs" and asked him what that stood for. "Black and Blue Boys," he replied with a smile, referring to the males of this genus. Unlike many damselflies, males remain colorful throughout life, as there is little tendency for the brilliant blues to darken or become obscured with pruinosity as they age. Males can sometimes be identified in the field by their color patterns, but firm identifications often require examination in the hand, especially for blue-type bluets (see below), where the distinctive shapes of their terminal appendages can be seen in side view with a hand lens (pgs. 58-59). **Even when color patterns seem sufficient to identify a species, it is always a good idea to confirm it by comparing the side view of the cerci and paraprocts with the drawings in this guide. If you get into the habit of doing this early, you won't regret it!**

To ease the task of identification with this large genus, I've grouped males into three subgroups: "black-type" bluets have the tops of the abdomens mostly black (especially the middle segments 3

through 5); "blue-type" bluets have abdomens with much blue (usually at least half blue on the middle segments); and "citrus-hued" bluets have the pale color either yellow or orange instead of blue. The Rainbow Bluet presents an exceptional case because of its green thorax and orange face (pg. 84). Female American bluets are duller than males in color, typically showing green, yellowish green or tan hues where the males are blue. Females of the blue-type bluets are often blacker on top of the

Black-type bluet.   **Blue-type bluet.**

abdomen than the males. Females of many species have male-like forms, which are usually less common than the typical heterochromatic form. Females can sometimes be identified in the hand, or even in the field, by distinctive color patterns, but some "clusters" of species are very similar, requiring careful examination of their mesostigmal plates under a microscope. Females of these species can often be identified (tentatively) by the males they are associated with. Females have a vulvar spine, contrasting with the Eurasian bluets, which lack the spine. Wings of both sexes are clear, moderately "stalked," and have dark stigmas, unless noted differently in the species accounts. Eyespots are always present and are helpful in identification because they vary in size among species. The tibial spurs are short, in contrast with the dancers.

These familiar, bright-blue damselflies often abound in grasses and sedges around ponds and lakes in early summer. Well-vegetated still-waters are the habitats of choice for most species, but other habitats are sometimes used, including streams and rivers. Most American bluets are weak fliers, making short forays close to vegetation after tiny insect prey, although some do fly strongly over water. Males do not usually defend territories or show much aggression toward other males. Females oviposit usually while in tandem but sometimes alone, into living or rotting plant stems or algal mats, sometimes while fully submerged.

The larvae are green or brown and of moderate build, with gills that are variable in shape, though usually narrow. The larvae are notoriously hard to identify. Ponds without sunfishes or black bass favor species of bluets that escape by swimming away (Azure Bluet, Boreal Bluet and Northern Bluet). Our other bluets do just fine in waters with fish. These species do not try to escape from fish predators by out-swimming them (a fruitless undertaking), but hide instead. All North Woods species overwinter as larvae.

This worldwide genus has more species in North America (at least 37 of them) than are found anywhere else. A diverse group of 14 species inhabits the North Woods. The phylogenetic status of a possible fifteenth species, the Vernal Bluet (*Enallagma cyathigerum vernale*), is presently being studied and vigorously debated among odonatists. Because the Vernal Bluet is very similar to the Northern Bluet, with which it intergrades extensively, I am considering them to be subspecies for now until more data about their morphology, habitat and genetic relationship become available. Look for two borderline species, the Western Slender Bluet and the Double-striped Bluet, to the south and east in the North Woods.

Orange Bluet *Enallagma signatum* (male)

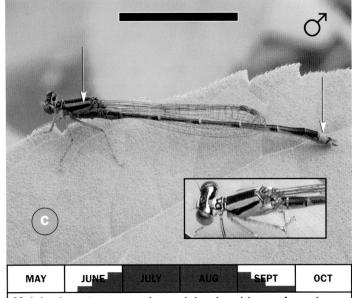

MAY	JUNE	JULY	AUG	SEPT	OCT

Mainly slow streams and marsh-bordered bays of ponds and lakes where it often flies low over open water.

Nature Notes:

Reaches greatest abundance in the latter part of summer after most bluets have declined.

Peak activity occurs late in the day, even toward dusk.

Description: Adults average 1.3 inches long. The male of this slender, citrus-hued bluet is a study in black and orange. On the thorax, the orange shoulder stripe (↑) is wider than the black one. The abdomen is mostly black with segment 9 entirely orange (↑). Eyes are orange and eyespots small. Female is dull yellow, pale green or blue where male is orange. Her abdomen is mostly dark except for segment 10 and the sides of segment 9, which are pale. Immature males are pale blue (see inset photo).

Identification Clues: Males are easily identified by their orange color, including the entire top of abdominal segment 9. On the female look for the following: pale shoulder stripe that is at least as wide as the dark stripe, entirely dark top of abdominal segment 8, pale top of segment 10 and pale sides of segment 9 (↑).

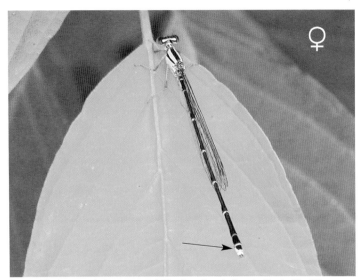

Orange Bluets are not always orange! Blue-form female Orange Bluets, like this one, are less common than those showing yellow or green.

Life Cycle: Adults emerge over a long period of at least two months beginning in mid June and flying well into September. Pairing and egg laying occur throughout the summer. Female, while in tandem, lays eggs into floating and emergent plants, with water lilies appearing to be favored. Overwinters as larvae in several late instars.

Tiger-stripe coloration of the male is unique among damselflies.

Vesper Bluet *Enallagma vesperum* (male)

♂

FC

| MAY | JUNE | JULY | AUG | SEPT | OCT |

Marsh-bordered lakes, ponds and slow rivers, usually well vegetated and often with water lilies.

Nature Notes:

Typically flies and mates well into the evening (hence its species name)—bring your flashlight to watch it happen!

May be more common in the North Woods than thought because of its crepuscular habits.

Flies low over the water, often landing on lily pads.

Description: Adults average 1.3 inches long.

The male of this slender citrus-hued bluet is beautiful and utterly unmistakable. Male thorax is bright yellow (↑) with the dark shoulder stripe very thin to nearly absent; abdomen is mostly black with segment 9 entirely blue (↑). Female is similar to the male, but her thorax is greenish yellow and the top of her abdomen is dark except for segment 10 and the sides of segment 9, which are pale blue or green.

Identification Clues: Males are easily identified by the combination of yellow thorax and blue abdomen tip. Note the black quadrangle on top of his abdominal segment 10 (↑). On the female look for the following: a pale shoulder stripe that is very thin or indistinct in middle (↑), entirely dark top of abdominal segment 8, a pale segment 10 and pale sides of segment 9.

imm. ♂

Male Vesper Bluets start adulthood pale blue, gaining the bright yellow thorax only at full maturity.

Life Cycle: Adults begin to emerge in June and have a long flight period that often extends into September. Egg laying occurs in the evening, while in tandem. Eggs are deposited into the leaves of water lilies and perhaps other floating or emergent plants. Overwinters as larvae in several late instars.

Note the male's black quadrangle on top of segment 10.

Rainbow Bluet *Enallagma antennatum* (male)

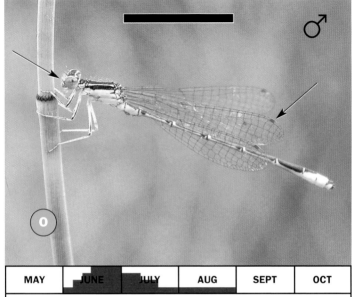

MAY	JUNE	JULY	AUG	SEPT	OCT

Quiet streams. Also springy margins of lakes and ponds especially near outlets.

Nature Notes:

Seeing this strikingly colored bluet for the first time is a notable experience!

Green thorax suggests a forktail more than a bluet, but none of our forktails have a similar color combination.

Description: Adults average 1.2 inches long.

Male is a black-type bluet with a green thorax, orange face and orange eyes (↑). The dark shoulder stripe is wide and the pale shoulder stripe is narrow and yellow. The top of abdominal segment 9 is entirely blue (↑). Female's thorax is similar, but greenish yellow (↑) where male's is green. Her abdomen is dark above with an elongate blue or green spot on top of segment 9. Both sexes have narrow eyespots. Wings clear with orange stigmas (↑).

Identification Clues: Male is unmistakable because of his rainbow combination of colors. Female's orange face and spindle-shaped blue spot on top of segment 9 are unique.

Life Cycle: Adults emerge from early June to mid July and fly through August. Pairing and egg laying occurs throughout July. While the pair is in tandem, the female will sometimes

The thin yellow shoulder stripes, small blue eyespots and orange stigmas are easy to spot on this female Rainbow Bluet.

descend below the water's surface to lay eggs into plant stems. Overwinters as a late-instar larva.

A male Rainbow showing off his rainbow colors. Note the all-blue segment 9.

Azure Bluet *Enallagma aspersum* (male)

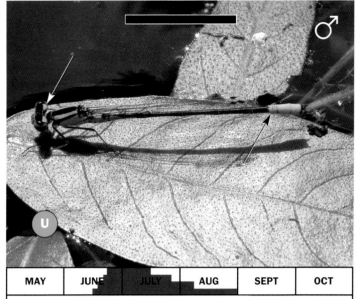

MAY	JUNE	JULY	AUG	SEPT	OCT

Shallow ponds and small lakes, sometimes boggy and usually lacking fish, including temporary and newly formed ponds.

Nature Notes:

Occurs at very few sites in the North Woods, but may be abundant once found.

Males aggressively attempt to drive other males from choice breeding sites.

Larvae sometimes found in ponds subject to periodic winterkill of fish.

Description: Adults average 1.2 inches long.

The male of this mid-sized, black-type bluet has a blue and black thorax with a narrow, dark shoulder stripe. Male's abdomen is mostly black above on segments 4 through 6, segments 8 and 9 are entirely blue and segment 7 is mostly blue (↑). Male's eyespots are very large (↑). The female is very similar to the male, except for her abdomen, which has paired blue spots on top of segments 8 (large spots) and 9 (small spots) (↑).

Identification Clues: The male is only black-type bluet in North Woods with segment 7 usually at least half blue. The female is the only North Woods bluet having paired blue spots on top of segments 7 and 8.

Life Cycle: Adults have a fairly long flight period, emerging in June and flying through August. Females oviposit alone or in tandem

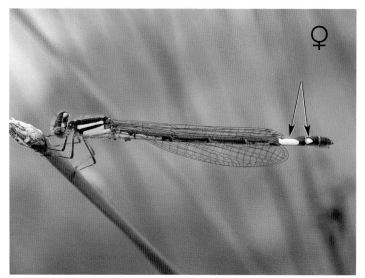

♀

The female Azure Bluet is one of the few American bluets to have only a blue form. Pairs of pale spots near the abdomen tip make these females easy to recognize in the field.

into submerged vegetation. Females may remain submerged for 25 minutes. Eggs hatch in about three weeks. Larvae live underwater for about a year and overwinter in one of the later instars.

Stream Bluet *Enallagma exsulans* (male)

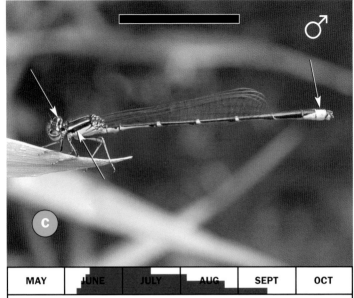

MAY	JUNE	JULY	AUG	SEPT	OCT

Flowing-water habitats from mid-sized streams to larger rivers; also sheltered lakeshores.

Nature Notes:

Perhaps the most common damselfly along streams and rivers in the North Woods.

Stream Bluets spend over an hour in copulation.

Often found in the company of dancers (the damselfly variety of dancers, that is).

Description: Adults average 1.3 inches long.

The male of this mid-sized, black-type bluet has a blue and black thorax with a dark shoulder stripe wider than the blue stripe (↑). Male's abdomen is mostly black above with segments 3 through 6 having thin blue rings at the bases and segment 9 is all blue (↑). The female is similarly marked, but is light green instead of blue on the thorax and the dark shoulder stripe is often divided in the middle with brown. Female shows abdominal segment 10 and much of segment 9 blue. Eyespots of both sexes are small and narrow (↑).

Identification Clues: The male is the only black-type bluet in the North Woods with a blue thorax and only abdominal segment 9 entirely blue. On female look for her light green thorax, wide black shoulder stripes divided by brown and the bluish abdomen tip.

A mating pair of Stream Bluets in the position called the wheel. The female is below.

Life Cycle: Emerges in June and is abundant by the end of the month. Remains abundant and pairing through July and into August. Some individuals fly through mid September. Females oviposit alone or in tandem into submerged aquatic plants and may descend well below the surface. Larvae overwinter in later instars.

Skimming Bluet *Enallagma geminatum* (male)

MAY	JUNE	JULY	AUG	SEPT	OCT

Larger ponds, lakes and slow streams, usually well-vegetated.

Nature Notes:

Flies low over lily pads and lands on them often, making them difficult to net.

Active in the middle of the day when light intensity is high.

Larvae evidently need clean, well-oxygenated water, perhaps to a greater extent than most damselfly species.

Description: Adults average 1 inch long.

A tiny, unmistakable black-type bluet. Male has a blue and black thorax with a thick, dark shoulder stripe and a blue shoulder stripe that may be constricted near the middle (↑). Male's abdomen is mostly black above on segments 2 through 7 (↑) with segments 8 and 9 all blue. Female is similar but with a pair of blue spots that may be fused on top of segment 8 (↑). Both sexes have a wavy blue line bordered above and below with black on the side of abdominal segment 2 (↑).

Identification Clues: Their tiny size and the wavy blue line on the side of abdominal segment 2 set both sexes apart from all other bluets.

Life Cycle: Emerges in June and flies throughout the summer, often into September. Females oviposit in tandem or

The female Skimming Bluet has a pair of blue spots on the top of abdominal segment 8.

alone, laying the eggs into emergent or floating vegetation including algae. Larvae overwinter in one of the later instars.

Note the distinctive wavy blue stripe bordered by black on this male's abdominal segment 2.

Tule Bluet *Enallagma carunculatum* (male)

MAY	JUNE	JULY	AUG	SEPT	OCT

Lakes, ponds and slow rivers, especially open shores of large lakes near bulrushes. Tolerates saline and brackish waters.

Nature Notes:

Often found at the open shores of larger, deeper lakes.

Tule Bluets have a long, mid-summer flight period in the North Woods.

Description: Adults average 1.3 inches long.

The male of this fairly large, blue-type bluet has a blue and black thorax with a dark shoulder stripe of moderately even width (↑). Male's abdomen is about half blue on segments 2 through 4 (↑) with increasing amounts of black on 5, 6 and 7; segments 8 and 9 are all blue. Female's pale areas are blue to olive-tan with her thorax markings similar to male's. The top of her abdomen is mostly dark but with pale markings at the bases of some segments. Eyespots rather small, especially on the female (↑).

Identification Clues: Male shows more black on his abdomen than other blue-type bluets and has smaller eyespots than Northern and Boreal Bluets. Terminal appendages seen in side view are unmistakable (pg. 59). Female cannot be reliably distinguished from several

Female Tule Bluets may be olive, tan or blue. Note this blue-form female's tiny eyespots.

other bluets except under a microscope.

Life Cycle: This species emerges from late June through July and flies into September. Emergence may occur high on rush stems, a foot above water. Females oviposit in tandem into stems of plants that are submerged or well above water. Egg laying may occur into autumn. Larvae live for nearly a year, have eight to 12 instars (usually ten) and overwinter in one of the later instars.

Hazards are everywhere in the North Woods. These two males are stuck to the flower head of a sow thistle.

Familiar Bluet *Enallagma civile* (male)

MAY	JUNE	JULY	AUG	SEPT	OCT

Wide variety of still-water habitats including lakes, ponds, marshes and bogs. Even in brackish and alkaline waters.

Nature Notes:

This notable disperser is expanding its range north into newly created habitats like mitigation marshes and wildlife ponds.

Males are peaceful to a fault—they do not compete for territories, nor do they court females or engage in displays of any kind. Even the species name means "polite."

Description: Adults average 1.3 inches long.

The male of this fairly large, blue-type bluet has a blue and black thorax with a narrow, dark shoulder stripe. Male's abdomen is mostly blue on segments 2 through 5 (↑) with black areas increasing on 6 and 7; segments 8 and 9 are all blue. Female's pale area is blue to olive-tan with her thorax markings similar to male's. The top of her abdomen is mostly dark, but with pale areas at the bases of some segments. Eyespots are moderately sized and tear-shaped (↑).

Identification Clues: Male is a bit larger than the Marsh and Hagen's Bluet and usually has less black on his abdomen than the Tule and Alkali Bluet. Northern and Boreal Bluets have larger eyespots. Terminal appendages seen in side view are unmistakable (pg. 59). Female cannot be reliably distinguished from several other bluets except under a microscope.

Female Familiar Bluets like this blue-form specimen are hard to separate from some Tule, Marsh and Hagen's Bluets.

Life Cycle: The Familiar Bluet has a very long and apparently bi-modal, flight period, with emergence peaks in June or early July and again in late August and September. Some individuals may fly into October. Females oviposit into plant stems first in tandem above the surface and then alone beneath the surface. Larvae live for nearly a year and overwinter in one of the later instars.

Note the tear-shaped eyespots and the blue shoulder stripe that is wider than the dark stripe.

River Bluet *Enallagma anna* (male)

MAY	JUNE	JULY	AUG	SEPT	OCT

Slow-flowing small to medium-sized streams; sometimes irrigation ditches in agricultural areas.

Nature Notes:

A western species that appears to have recently extended its range to the east.

May hybridize with other closely related bluets.

Carefully examine blue-type bluets along streams in the North Woods for this uncommon species.

Found at higher elevations out West.

Description: Adults average 1.3 inches long.

A robust, blue-type bluet. Male has a blue and black thorax with a dark shoulder stripe narrowing rearward (↑). Male's abdomen has segments 2 through 5 mostly blue, 6 and 7 mostly black and segments 8 and 9 all blue. Female shows pale areas of blue or olive with narrow dark shoulder stripes and a mostly dark top of abdomen. Both sexes have eyespots of moderate size (↑).

Identification Clues: Male is similar to other blue-type bluets with narrow dark stripes, but is readily identified in the hand by the long, distinctively shaped cerci (pg. 59). Female is very similar to Boreal and Northern Bluets and can only be identified with certainty under a microscope.

Female River Bluets may be all blue, as this one, or partially or entirely olive.

Life Cycle: Little is known about the ecology and reproduction of this species in the North Woods. Adults fly primarily in June and July. The larvae are unusual among bluets because they live in streams where they overwinter in later instars.

Pair of River Bluets ovipositing in a stream. Female is depositing eggs while the male contact-guards her.

Alkali Bluet *Enallagma clausum* (male)

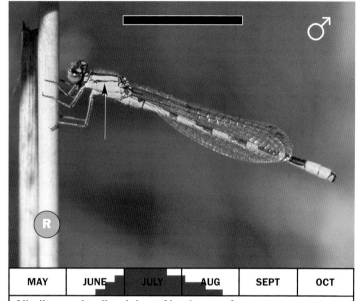

MAY	JUNE	JULY	AUG	SEPT	OCT

Alkaline and saline lakes. Also known from wave-swept shores of large freshwater lakes.

Nature Notes:

An uncommon species in the North Woods but recently discovered in Wisconsin along the Lake Superior shore.

Flies alertly and low over open beaches and can be hard to catch.

Description: Adults average 1.3 inches long.

The male of this mid-sized, blue-type bluet has a blue and black thorax with a narrow dark shoulder stripe (↑). Male's abdomen with increasing amounts of black on segments 2 through 7; segments 8 and 9 are all blue. Female's pale areas are blue to yellowish green with her thorax markings similar to the male's. The top of her abdomen is mostly dark, but with segment 8 entirely pale (↑). Eyespots of both sexes moderate in size.

Identification Clues: Separate male from Boreal and Northern Bluets in the hand by looking for the short, downward-angled cerci in side view (pg. 59). On females, look for the entirely pale segment 8 (but note that female Boreal Bluets can also have a pale segment 8). Firm identifications require seeing mesostigmal plates under a microscope.

The female Alkali Bluet is similar to the Boreal and Northern Bluets, all of which have thin, dark shoulder stripes and can have extensive pale areas on top of abdominal segment 8. However, the Alkali is most likely to have the top of that segment entirely pale.

Life Cycle: Little is known about this species in the North Woods. Flight period appears to be concentrated during mid-summer, with most adults taken here in July. Females oviposit in tandem into masses of filamentous algae and perhaps other vegetation. Larvae overwinter in one of the later instars.

Boreal Bluet *Enallagma boreale* (male)

MAY	JUNE	JULY	AUG	SEPT	OCT

Still-water habitats: shallow, well-vegetated ponds, marshy lake-shores, prairie sloughs, bogs. Tolerant of acidic conditions.

Nature Notes:

The first bluet and one of the earliest damselflies to emerge in the North Woods.

One of the most abundant damselflies in the Far North.

When a larva loses a leg, it is able to regenerate a new nearly normal one.

Larvae survive best in ponds that lack fish.

Description: Adults average 1.3 inches long. A fairly large, blue-type bluet. Male has a blue and black thorax with a dark shoulder stripe narrowing rearward (↑). Male's abdomen has segments 2 through 5 mostly blue, 6 and 7 mostly black and segments 8 and 9 all blue. Female has pale areas light blue to olive or tan with thorax markings similar to male. The top of her abdomen is mostly dark with a pair of blue spots of variable size on top of segment 8 (↑) (often fused). Both sexes have fairly large eyespots; the male's nearly touch the eye (↑).

Identification Clues: Very similar to the Northern Bluet, from which it can be separated only in the hand by viewing the shape of cerci in side view (pg. 59). Female can only be separated from other bluets with narrow, dark-shoulder stripes under a microscope.

Female Boreal Bluets may be blue-form, like this one, or olive-tan. This species is similar to the Northern and Alkali Bluets, all of which have thin dark shoulder stripes and can have extensive pale areas on top of abdominal segment 8.

Life Cycle: Emerges and flies early, reaching peak abundance in June. Females oviposit either in tandem or alone into emergent plant stems above the water's surface. Larvae live underwater for about a year and overwinter in one of the later instars.

Northern Bluet *Enallagma cyathigerum* (male)

MAY	JUNE	JULY	AUG	SEPT	OCT

Well-vegetated shallow ponds, marshes and vernal pools.
Also found in some bogs and fens.

Nature Notes:

While laying eggs, the female may stay underwater for 90 minutes!

Larvae survive best in ponds that lack fish.

Very similar to the Boreal Bluet but appears a bit later in the season than that species and may be less tolerant of acidic conditions.

Description: Adults average 1.3 inches long.

The male of this mid-sized, blue-type bluet has a blue and black thorax with a narrow, dark shoulder stripe (↑). Male's abdomen has segments 2 through 5 mostly blue, 6 and 7 mostly black and segments 8 and 9 all blue. Female's pale areas are light blue to yellowish green with thorax markings similar to male's. The top of her abdomen is mostly dark, often with a pair of pale spots of variable size on top of segment 8 (↑). Both sexes have large eyespots; the male's nearly touch the eye.

Identification Clues: Male is very similar to the Boreal Bluet and can only be separated from that species by viewing the shape of cerci in side view (pg. 59). Female can only be separated from other female bluets with narrow, dark-shoulder stripes under a microscope.

The female Northern Bluet is similar to the Boreal and Alkali Bluets, all of which have thin, dark shoulder stripes and can have extensive pale areas on top of abdominal segment 8.

The Vernal Bluet (*Enallagma cyathigerum vernale*) is a closely related subspecies, differing in subtle aspects of the male cerci and perhaps in habitat and habits. It may eventually be found to be deserving of full-species status. Although the Vernal Bluet has been found at a few sites in northern Wisconsin, it has not been looked for widely in the North Woods and its status here is unclear.

Life Cycle: Emerges and flies early, reaching peak abundance in June and early July. Females lay eggs into vegetation while in tandem near the surface, or alone into submerged plant stems while males guard nearby. Female may remain submerged for 90 minutes! Larvae live underwater for about a year and overwinter in one of the later instars.

Marsh Bluet *Enallagma ebrium* (male)

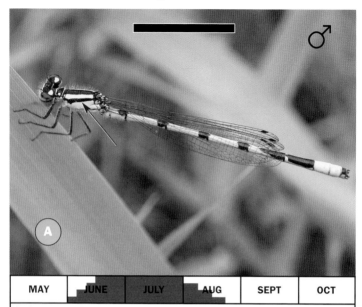

MAY	JUNE	JULY	AUG	SEPT	OCT

Lakes, ponds, marshes and slow streams that have marshy borders. Most abundant in waters on calcareous soils.

Nature Notes:

Species name means "drunken," perhaps due to its occasionally erratic flight.

Virtually identical to Hagen's Bluet (except for male's cerci), but does not tolerate acidic conditions like that species does.

Description: Adults average 1.1 inches long.

The male of this small, blue-type bluet has a blue and black thorax with a dark shoulder stripe of moderate width (↑). Male's abdomen is mostly blue on segments 2 through 5 with increasing areas of black on 6 and 7; segments 8 and 9 are all blue. Female's thorax is similar to male's, but may be light green, tan or even blue where he is blue. Her abdomen is all dark above (↑). Eyespots of both sexes moderate in size.

Identification Clues: Male is most like Hagen's bluet, but differs in having distinctive cerci with two arms about equal in length (pg. 59). Female Marsh and Hagen's Bluets differ from all other bluets by having the top of the abdomen entirely black, but can only be reliably separated from each other under a microscope.

Note that the top of the female Marsh Bluet's abdomen is entirely dark on all segments. This trait is shared only with the female Hagen's Bluet.

Life Cycle: Emerges in June over a three-week period and flies through the middle of August. Pairing and egg laying begin in late June and continue through July. Females oviposit alone or in tandem into floating plants, dead or alive, or plants stems below the surface, sometimes becoming fully submerged by a foot or more. Larvae overwinter in one of the later instars.

Hagen's Bluet *Enallagma hageni* (male)

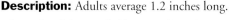

MAY	JUNE	JULY	AUG	SEPT	OCT

Well-vegetated ponds, marshes and bogs. Tolerant of acidic conditions.

Nature Notes:

One of the most abundant summer damselflies in the North Woods.

Males are almost identical to the Marsh Bluet. Compare terminal appendages to separate them.

Description: Adults average 1.2 inches long.
The male of this small, blue-type bluet has a blue and black thorax with a dark shoulder stripe of moderate width (↑). Male's abdomen is mostly blue on segments 2 through 5 with increasing areas of black on 6 and 7; segments 8 and 9 are all blue. Female's thorax is similar to male's, but may be light green or tan where he is blue. The top of her abdomen is entirely dark (↑). Eyespots of both sexes are moderate in size.

Identification Clues: Male is most like the Marsh Bluet, but differs in the shape of its cerci, which have a single horizontal arm (pg. 59). Female Marsh and Hagen's Bluets differ from all other bluets by having the top of the abdomen entirely black, but can only be reliably separated from each other under a microscope.

This blue-form female Hagen's Bluet is atypical; most are pale green or tan. Note that the top of her abdomen is entirely dark on all segments. This trait is shared only with the female Marsh Bluet.

Life Cycle: Emerges in June and flies into September. Pairing and egg laying begin in late June and continue through July. Females oviposit in tandem into floating plants, dead or alive, or stems just below the surface, without becoming fully submerged. Eggs hatch in about three weeks. Larvae live for nearly a year and overwinter in one of the later instars.

This immature male does not yet show the bright blue of the adults.

Forktails
Genus *Ischnura*

Forktails are small, strikingly patterned damselflies that are similar in appearance to the American bluets (genus *Enallagma*) and the Eurasian bluets (genus *Coenagrion*). However, their clear wings, the variation in color of females and the small forked structure at the tip of the abdomen of males set the genus apart from other closely related groups. The stigmas of the males differ in size or color between the fore- and hindwings, except in the Fragile Forktail. Females in this genus appear to come in a bewildering array of colors for two reasons. First, some species have a male-like form (homeochromatic): this tendency is rare in the Eastern Forktail, unknown in the Citrine Forktail but is the only form found in the Fragile Forktail. Then, to add to the confusion, females change color as they age, either by darkening or with a grayish-white or bluish pruinescence gradually obscuring much or all of the underlying color pattern. But the signature feature of the forktails is exactly that—the forked projection on top of abdominal segment 10 that the famous odonatist E. M. Walker aptly called a "turret-like eminence, which is more or less distinctly bi-lobed." The scientific name *Ischnura* means "slender-tailed," referring to their slender abdomen.

In addition to their distinctive appearance, forktails also have some unusual life history features that set them apart from other groups. Our species have long flight periods; emerging in the spring and flying throughout the summer. Newly emerged forktails reach reproductive maturity more rapidly than other damselflies, sometimes in just one day. Females of some species may mate only once (unusual for damselflies) and females of all of our species usually oviposit alone. Forktails are feeble fliers that hold close to the emergent vegetation along the shoreline of their breeding habitat.

This abundant genus of pond damsels is found throughout the world in still-water habitats. There are 14 species in North America, of which three are residents of the North Woods. The Eastern Forktail is one of our most abundant and widespread damselflies, while the other two species are uncommon. Three additional species, the Plains Forktail, Lilypad Forktail and Western Forktail, range close to the southern and western edges of the North Woods and are worth keeping an eye open for. Males are readily identified in the field by their distinctive colors and patterns; none of our species looks particularly like either of the others. Identifications can be confirmed by viewing the terminal appendages with a hand lens. Identifying females can often be done in the field by their distinctive color patterns, but the pruinescence on older females largely obscures these patterns. Identification of problematic females can only be done with certainty by carefully examining their mesostigmal plates under a microscope.

Eastern Forktail *Ischnura verticalis* (male)

MAY	JUNE	JULY	AUG	SEPT	OCT

Wide array of permanent still waters including ponds, lake bays, marshes and slow streams.

Nature Notes:

One of the most widely distributed and abundant damselflies in the North Woods.

Females often flutter their wings at males, but this seems to be more of a threat than a courtship display.

Description: Adults average 1.2 inches long.

A small, dark and strikingly marked species. Male's pale shoulder stripe and lower thorax are green and the tip of his abdomen is blue. His head is dark with small, bright green eye-spots. Younger female's rear of head, most of thorax and base of abdomen are all orange. She has a black, thin shoulder stripe, black mid-dorsal stripe and most of her abdomen is black. Females turn entirely bluish pruinose with age, but the complete shoulder stripes may remain visible.

Identification Clues: Look for the square, dark spots (↑) on the sides of the blue abdomen tip of male (segments 8 and 9). Females have complete pale and dark shoulder stripes and a small vulvar spine (no other North Woods forktail has this combination).

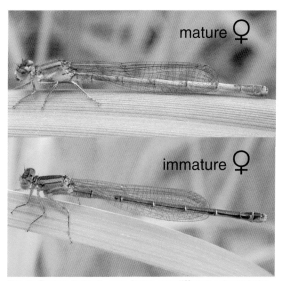

Female Eastern Forktails come in two very different color varieties. Immatures are orange and turn bluish-gray pruinose with age.

Life Cycle: Adults begin to emerge in late May and continue to emerge throughout the summer. Some individuals may still be flying in October. Adults mature in about ten days after emergence, but do not fly far from the breeding site. Females may only mate once, which is unusual for damselflies. Females oviposit alone (usually) into submerged aquatic plants. Larvae progress through 11 to 13 instars and overwinter in various instars.

Rarely, the male Eastern Forktail shows a divided shoulder stripe much like the Fragile Forktail.

Fragile Forktail *Ischnura posita* (male)

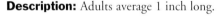

MAY	JUNE	JULY	AUG	SEPT	OCT

Slow streams and ponds that are shaded, heavily vegetated and often spring-fed.

Nature Notes:

One of our most shade-tolerant damselflies.

Species name means "positive," probably alluding to the exclamation point on the thorax!

Description: Adults average 1 inch long.

Very small, dark species. Male's thorax and abdomen are black above with a pale green shoulder stripe interrupted to form a dot and short line like an exclamation point (!) (↑). Very thin, pale rings around the base of each abdominal segment. Female is very similar, but may have pale blue (↑) or green on her thorax. Female is never orange. She turns grayish with age, but the interrupted shoulder stripe usually remains visible.

Identification Clues: Both sexes are readily identified in the field by pale shoulder stripe divided like an exclamation point. Male's dark top of the abdomen (↑) is unique; males of all other North Woods pond damsels have at least one entirely pale segment on top of their abdomen (pale segment may be blue, green, red, orange or yellow).

Female Fragile Forktails are patterned much like the males but they may have blue on the thorax shading to gray with age.

Life Cycle: Adults have a long flight period from late May well into September. Females oviposit into stems of emergent vegetation. Life history and reproduction of this species have not been well studied. Probably overwinters in one of the final larval instars.

Note the pair of divided shoulder stripes like tiny exclamation points. The Fragile Forktail is the only North Woods damselfly to always show this mark. Eastern Forktails rarely do but they never have the dark abdomen top.

Citrine Forktail *Ischnura hastata* (male)

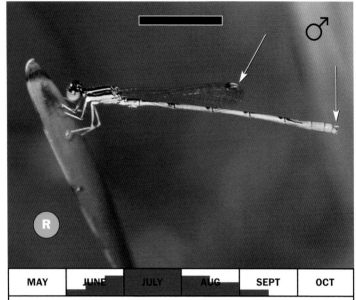

MAY	JUNE	JULY	AUG	SEPT	OCT

Permanent but small wet areas of spring seepage, often thickly overgrown with spike rush or club-rushes.

Nature Notes:

Called "exquisite little creatures" by pioneering odonatists Needham and Heywood.

Along with the Sphagnum Sprite, one of the tiniest damselflies in the North Woods and also one of the rarest.

Hard to see in their densely-vegetated habitats.

Description: Adults average 0.9 inches long.

Tiny yellow and black damselfly. Male has a dark top of the head with tiny blue-green eye-spots. Thorax is dark above and yellowish-green below with thin pale shoulder stripes. Abdomen is largely yellowish-orange with regularly spaced dark marks. When viewed from above, the tip of the abdomen shows a very prominent two-pronged fork (↑). Young females are orange with dark marks on top of the thorax and on top of abdominal segments 6 through 9. Females darken with age, becoming increasingly bluish-gray with some pruinosity.

Identification Clues: The male is easily recognized in the field by his small size and mostly yellowish-orange abdomen. Orange stigma in forewing of male is unique in being well separated from the wing margin (↑).

♀

This specimen shows the heavy bluish-gray pruinosity of an older female Citrine Forktail. When at this stage, they are difficult to separate from other female forktails.

Look for the very thin or absent shoulder stripe (↑) on young (orange) females; older females are difficult to separate from other forktails although the lack of a dark shoulder stripe may remain evident.

Life Cycle: Adult flight period is fairly long, from early June into September. Females oviposit alone into stems of emergent vegetation. Life history and reproduction of this species have not been well studied. Probably overwinters in one of the final larval instars.

Note the very thin, dark shoulder stripe and overall orange color of this young female.

Sprites
Genus *Nehalennia*

The sprites are tiny, dainty damselflies that are easy to identify once you find their haunts. Their small size, unstriped metallic-green thorax and lack of eyespots sets them apart at a glance from all other damselflies. Sprites typically fly low among plants and are reluctant to fly over open water. For this reason and because they are so small, they are inconspicuous and require a bit of patience to observe. Once you find them, they are fun to watch and will often allow you to approach quite closely. These fragile insects are both beautiful and interesting. The name *Nehalennia*, appropriately enough, is after a river goddess of the Rhein. I've noticed that when shown their first sprite, people often respond by saying, "How cute!" or "Isn't it adorable!"

Six species of sprites are known from around the world, five from the Americas and just two species are found in the North Woods. Sedge Sprites are very common and widespread in a variety of habitats, whereas Sphagnum Sprites are rare and limited to the sphagnum moss margins around bog ponds. Identifying the two species requires determining the gender first, which can be a challenge with such a dainty subject! Males can be identified in the field based on the pattern of blue on abdominal segments 8 to 10. Females are best identified in the hand by the shape of the rear edge of the prothorax.

Females in this genus oviposit in tandem in floating bits of dead rushes or other vegetation, or into moist sphagnum moss. The female keeps her body horizontal when egg laying as the contact-guarding male supports himself at a 45 degree angle by holding her prothorax with his claspers.

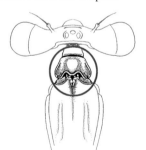
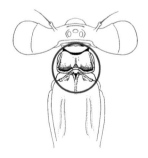

Female Sedge Sprite prothorax: note three-lobed hind margin.

Female Sphagnum Sprite prothorax: note two-lobed hind margin.

Sphagnum Sprite *Nehalennia gracilis* (male)

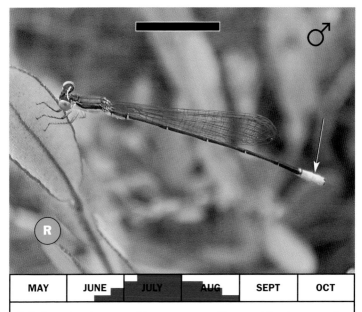

♂

R

MAY	JUNE	JULY	AUG	SEPT	OCT

Only in wet sphagnum fringes surrounding quaking bog ponds.

Description: Adults average 0.9 inches long. Eyes blue, face pale blue. No eyespots, but a thin blue bar is usually present along the back of the head. The thorax and abdomen are unstriped, metallic green on the top half, light blue below. Females and tenerals are yellowish below. Abdominal segments 9 and 10 of male are entirely pale blue (↑) and segment 8 is mostly blue with a small dark area at base. Female lacks vulvar spine.

Identification Clues: Segments 9 and 10 of male are all blue whereas male Sedge Sprite has small dark areas at the base of both segments. Rear edge of prothorax of female has two wide lobes while female Sedge Sprite has three distinct lobes (see illustration on pg. 116).

Life Cycle: Adults emerge in June and fly into late August. Life-history studies have not been done for the Sphagnum Sprite.

Nature Notes:

This eastern species is rare in the North Woods. However, it has hardly been looked for in its bog pond habitat at the western edge of its range. Might it be more common here than we think?

One of our daintiest damselflies. Species name comes from its slender abdomen.

Sedge Sprite *Nehalennia irene* (male)

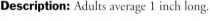

(A)

♂

| MAY | JUNE | JULY | AUG | SEPT | OCT |

Bogs, sedge fens, marshes, ponds, slow streams, some lakes and vernal pools.

Nature Notes:

Perhaps the most abundant damselfly in the North Woods.

Look for it flying low amongst the dense vegetation surrounding almost any still-water wetland that supports emergent plants.

Description: Adults average 1 inch long.

Eyes blue, face pale blue. No eyespots, but a thin blue bar is usually present along the back of the head. The thorax and abdomen are unstriped, metallic green on the top half, light blue below. Females and tenerals are yellowish below. Abdominal segments 9 and 10 of male are pale blue with dark areas at bases of the segments (↑). Vulvar spine lacking or tiny in female.

Identification Clues: Segments 9 and 10 of male blue with dark areas at the base of both segments. Male Sphagnum Sprite has segments 9 and 10 entirely blue. Rear edge of prothorax of female has three distinct lobes while female Sphagnum Sprite has only two wide lobes (see illustration on pg. 116).

Life Cycle: Adults emerge in late May or June and often fly throughout the summer.

Female Sedge Sprites are very similar in color to males but she lacks the blue markings of segments 8 and 9.

Eggs are laid in floating bits of dead plant material from about mid June through early August. Life-history information is scanty for this species. Larvae hatch a few days after egg laying and then progress through 12 or 13 molts. Overwinters in one of the final two larval instars and emerges the following spring.

Female laying eggs as the male contact-guards her.

Tiny size, metallic-green thorax and blue eyes immediately indicate a sprite.

Rare Strays to the North Woods

The following seven species do not regularly occur in the North Woods but live around its periphery. None of them are rare in their home range, but they are notable finds in the North Woods. A species range is not set in stone, but may move over time in response to environmental changes like global warming or the loss of habitat. Natural resource managers need to know about such changes, and tracking these borderline species is one way to do that. So, keep your eyes open and report sightings to the Odonata survey in your state or province (see Appendix B. Damselfly Groups & Websites).

Smoky Rubyspot *Hetaerina titia*

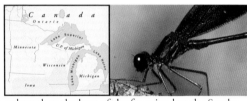

This large, dark rubyspot is a south-eastern species that favors rivers and streams with moderate current. Like the American Rubyspot, the male has a bright, red patch at the base of the forewing but the Smoky Rubyspot is darker, more slender and has dark wing tips. Watch for this handsome species along the southern edge of the North Woods.

Prairie Bluet *Coenagrion angulatum*

A northern and western species that is common in sunlit ponds and sloughs of the Canadian prairie. Look for it along the western edge of the North Woods. The male is similar to the Taiga Bluet, with green-bottomed eyes, but with more black on abdominal segments 3 through 5. Its abdomen is almost, but not quite, as black as a black-type bluet. Top of segment 2 has a thin, rearward curving black mark that looks something like a moustache.

Double-striped Bluet *Enallagma basidens*

This small, easily identified, blue-type bluet is common and widely distributed south and east of the North Woods. Recently it has been expanding its range to the north and west, so do keep your eyes open for it. Both sexes are unique among bluets in having the dark shoulder stripe narrowly divided along its entire length, with a thin pale stripe showing in between.

Western Slender Bluet *Enallagma traviatum westfalli*

This black-type bluet favors well-vegetated shorelines at the southern and eastern edges of our area. Males have very large eyespots, narrow black shoulder stripes, the top of abdominal segments 8 and 9 entirely blue and a very slender build. The terminal appendages of the male are most like the Azure Bluet and the River Bluet. However, the Azure Bluet has the top of segment 7 largely blue and River Bluet is a blue-type bluet.

Plains Forktail *Ischnura damula*

Small and dark, this forktail inhabits lakes and ponds just to the west of the North Woods and could easily show up along our western periphery. Males are easily recognized by the top of the thorax being extensively black, with the pale stripes reduced to four, small blue dots. The abdomen is dark with a blue tip.

Lilypad Forktail *Ischnura kellicotti*

As its name suggests, the life cycle of this distinctive southeastern species is closely tied to the presence of water lilies. Look for it at heavily vegetated ponds along the southern periphery of the North Woods. Males could be mistaken for a black-type bluet with a wide, black shoulder stripe and blue on top of abdominal segments 8 and 9. However, a blue ring at the base of segment 2 is a distinguishing mark.

Western Forktail *Ischnura perparva*

Like the Plains Forktail, this species inhabits ponds just to the west of the North Woods. The Western Forktail closely resembles the abundant Eastern Forktail, but it can be identified by its C-shaped lower clasper (paraproct). So, when you're damselflying at the western edge of our area, take an extra careful look at some male forktails with your hand lens.

Glossary

Antehumeral stripe: Pale stripe on side of the thorax between the dark middorsal stripe and the dark humeral stripe. Commonly called the pale shoulder stripe.

Cerci: (singular: cercus) Upper pair of the terminal appendages (claspers) of the male.

Claspers: Common term for the terminal appendages (cerci and paraprocts) of the male that are used to grasp the prothorax of the female during mating (a.k.a. caudal appendages).

Endophytic oviposition: Laying eggs inside of plant tissue.

Exuviae: Shed skin left behind when the larva climbs out of the water and transforms into the adult (the Latin source word has only the plural form, but some odonatists use a singular form exuvia to avoid ambiguity).

Heterochromatic: Female coloration not resembling the male.

Homeochromatic: Female coloration resembling the male.

Humeral stripe: Dark stripe on side of the thorax below the pale antehumeral stripe. Commonly called the dark shoulder stripe.

Larva: (plural: larvae) Immature aquatic stage of the damselfly. Sometimes called nymph or naiad.

Mesostigmal plates: Small sclerites at the front and top of the pterothorax that are often modified in females for contact with the male claspers when in tandem. Sometimes called "shoulder pads".

Middorsal stripes: Stripes that are usually dark that flank the middorsal carina on each side.

Nodus: Shallow notch on the leading edge of the wing where the two anterior wings veins (the costa and the subcosta) come together.

Occipital bar: Pale, transverse line found along the back of the head of some damselflies between the postocular spots (eyespots).

Ocelli: Three simple eyes found on top of an adult damselfly's head.

Odonatist/Odonatologist: A person who studies dragonflies and damselflies.

Oviposition: The act of laying eggs, which the female may do alone or accompanied by the male.

Ovipositor: The structure on the bottom side of the abdomen at segments 8 and 9 that the female damselfly uses to pierce an appropriate substrate and deposit eggs.

Paraprocts: The lower pair of terminal appendages (claspers) of the male (a.k.a. inferior appendages).

Pharate adult: Newly formed adult that has not yet emerged from the larval skin.

Postocular spots: Pale colored spots on top of the head near the eyes, sometimes connected to the occipital bar (a.k.a. eyespots).

Prothorax: The first segment of the thorax, which has no wings but has the first pair of legs.

Pruinosity: A whitish, grayish or pale bluish, waxy substance (bloom) that exudes from the cuticle as some damselflies mature. It may cover much of the body of an older adult (a.k.a. pruinescence).

Pseudostigma: Area of contrasting color at front tip of the wing near where a true stigma would be found, but often larger than a true stigma and containing multiple cells.

Pterothorax: The combined middle (meso-) and hind (meta-) parts of the thorax that are fused together for strength. Bears the wings and two pairs of legs (a.k.a. synthorax).

Stigma: Single cell near the tip of the wing that contrasts in color and texture with the rest of the wing (a.k.a. pterostigma).

Tandem: Position in which the male is holding the thorax of the female with his terminal appendages, but the pair is not copulating.

Teneral: young adult damselfly just after it has emerged from the larval stage but before its wings and sclerites are fully hardened and it is full colored (not yet sexually mature).

Vulvar spine: Sharp, pointed extension at the bottom end of abdominal segment 8 on females of some damselflies.

Wheel: The circular or heart-shaped position of mating damselflies when in tandem and with the female engaging the males secondary genitalia with the tip of her abdomen.

Zygoptera: The suborder of Odonata containing the damselflies.

Appendix A
Checklist of North Woods Damselflies

BROAD-WINGED DAMSELS Family Calopterygidae

Jewelwings
❏ River Jewelwing   *Calopteryx aequabilis*   C
❏ Ebony Jewelwing   *Calopteryx maculata*   A

Rubyspots
❏ American Rubyspot   *Hetaerina americana*   O
❏ Smokey Rubyspot   *Hetaerina titia*   VR

SPREADWINGS Family Lestidae

Spreadwings
❏ Amber-winged Spreadwing   *Lestes eurinus*   O
❏ Elegant Spreadwing   *Lestes inaequalis*   U
❏ Swamp Spreadwing   *Lestes vigilax*   FC
❏ Emerald Spreadwing   *Lestes dryas*   FC
❏ Slender Spreadwing   *Lestes rectangularis*   C
❏ Lyre-tipped Spreadwing   *Lestes unguiculatus*   O
❏ Sweetflag Spreadwing   *Lestes forcipatus*   FC
❏ Northern Spreadwing   *Lestes disjunctus*   C
❏ Spotted Spreadwing   *Lestes congener*   C

POND DAMSELS Family Coenagrionidae

Dancers
❏ Violet Dancer   *Argia fumipennis violacea*   C
❏ Powdered Dancer   *Argia moesta*   C
❏ Blue-fronted Dancer   *Argia apicalis*   FC
❏ Blue-tipped Dancer   *Argia tibialis*   FC

Eastern Red Damsel
❏ Eastern Red Damsel   *Amphiagrion saucium*   O

Aurora Damsel
❏ Aurora Damsel   *Chromagrion conditum*   FC

Eurasian Bluets
❏ Taiga Bluet   *Coenagrion resolutum*   FC
❏ Subarctic Bluet   *Coenagrion interrogatum*   R
❏ Prairie Bluet   *Coenagrion angulatum*   VR

American Bluets
(Citrus-hued Bluets)
❏ Orange Bluet   *Enallagma signatum*   C
❏ Vesper Bluet   *Enallagma vesperum*   FC

(Black-type Bluets)
❏ Rainbow Bluet   *Enallagma antennatum*   O
❏ Azure Bluet   *Enallagma aspersum*   U
❏ Stream Bluet   *Enallagma exsulans*   C
❏ Skimming Bluet   *Enallagma geminatum*   FC
❏ Western Slender Bluet   *Enallagma traviatum westfalli*   VR

(Blue-type Bluets)
❏ Tule Bluet   *Enallagma carunculatum*   C
❏ Familiar Bluet   *Enallagma civile*   FC
❏ River Bluet   *Enallagma anna*   U
❏ Alkali Bluet   *Enallagma clausum*   R
❏ Boreal Bluet   *Enallagma boreale*   C
❏ Northern Bluet   *Enallagma cyathigerum*   C
❏ Marsh Bluet   *Enallagma ebrium*   A
❏ Hagen's Bluet   *Enallagma hageni*   A
❏ Double-striped Bluet   *Enallagma basidens*   VR

Forktails
❏ Eastern Forktail   *Ischnura verticalis*   A
❏ Fragile Forktail   *Ischnura posita*   U
❏ Citrine Forktail   *Ischnura hastata*   R
❏ Lilypad Forktail   *Ischnura kellicotti*   VR
❏ Plains Forktail   *Ischnura damula*   VR
❏ Western Forktail   *Ischnura perparva*   VR

Sprites
❏ Sphagnum Sprite   *Nehalennia gracilis*   R
❏ Sedge Sprite   *Nehalennia irene*   A

A – Abundant	Hard to miss. Widespread and abundant.
C – Common	Encountered often and in many habitats.
FC – Fairly Common	Fairly easy to find on a given day.
O – Occasional	May be locally common but not widespread.
U – Uncommon	Never numerous. Must be in right habitat.
R – Rare	Right time and right habitat may equal success.
VR – Very Rare	Strays to our area. Lucky to see one ever.

Appendix B & C
Damselfly Groups & Websites

Wisconsin Odonata Survey (WOS)
Information about, and receives records of, Odonata in Wisconsin.
http://atriweb.info/Inventory/Odonata/Survey.cfm
(or at google.com type "wisconsin odonata survey")

International Odonata Research Institute
Comprehensive source for Odonata websites, collecting resources and
dragonfly books. Contact information for the world's odonatists.
IORI c/o Florida Div. of Plant Industry, 1911 SW 34th St., Gainesville FL 32608
http://www.afn.org/~iori/
(or at google.com type "odonata information network")

Michigan Odonata Survey
MOS c/o Museum of Zoology, Insect Division, University of Michigan, Ann
Arbor, MI 48109-1079. The MOS publishes the newsletter *Williamsonia*.
http://insects.ummz.lsa.umich.edu/MICHODO/MOS.html
(or at google.com type "michigan odonata survey")

Worldwide Dragonfly Association
Publishes the international journal *Pantala* and a newsletter, *Agrion*.
http://powell.colgate.edu/wda/dragonfly.html (or google "world dragonfly")

Dragonfly Society of the Americas
DSA publishes the journal *American Odonatology* and a newsletter, *Argia*.
http://www.afn.org/~iori/dsaintro.html (or google "dragonfly society americas")

Dragonflies and Damselflies of Ontario
Information about county distributions of Odonata in Ontario.
http://www.mnr.gov.on.ca/MNR/nhic/odonates/ohs.html
(or at google.com type "ontario odonata atlas")

Photo Credits

Mike Reese (mikereese@wisconsinbutterflies.org): All photos are
by Mike Reese except those noted below.

Bob DuBois (stormieblizzard@charter.net): 47m, 55b, 60 inset, 89

Sid Dunkle (SDunkle@ccccd.edu): 40, 41, 67, 75, 76, 77, 78
right, 98, 99, 103, 114, 115tb, 120 all, 121 all

Michael Furtman (www.michaelfurtman.com): 12b

Kurt Mead (mndfly@cpinternet.com): 29

Sparky Stensaas (sparkystensaas@hotmail.com): 1, 5, 8, 13tb, 63b,
110 inset

t=top, m=middle, b=bottom

Appendix D
Titles of Interest

Acorn, J. 2004. *Damselflies of Alberta: Flying Neon Toothpicks in the Grass.* Edmonton, AB: The University of Alberta Press.

Carpenter, V. 1991. *Dragonflies and Damselflies of Cape Cod.* Cape Cod Museum of Natural History. Natural History Series #4.

Corbet, P. S. 1999. *Dragonflies, Behavior and Ecology of Odonata.* Ithaca, NY: Cornell University Press.

Dunkle, S. W. 1990. *Damselflies of Florida, Bermuda, and the Bahamas.* Gainesville, FL: Scientific Publishers.

Glotzhober, R. C., and D. McShaffrey. 2002. *The Dragonflies and Damselflies of Ohio.* Columbus, OH: Ohio Biological Survey.

Holder, M. 1996. *The Dragonflies and Damselflies of Algonquin Provincial Park.* Algonquin Park Tech. Bulletin #11.

Lam, E. 2004. *Damselflies of the Northeast.* Forest Hills, NY: Biodiversity Books.

Mead, K. 2003. *Dragonflies of the North Woods.* Duluth, MN: Kollath-Stensaas Publishing.

Needham, J. G., M. J. Westfall and M. L. May. 2000. *Dragonflies of North America.* Gainesville, FL: Scientific Publishers, Inc.

Nikula, B., and J. Sones. 2002. *Stokes Beginner's Guide to Dragonflies.* Boston, MA: Little, Brown and Company.

Nikula, B., J. L. Loose, and M. R. Burne. 2003. *A Field Guide to the Dragonflies and Damselflies of Massachusetts.* Westborough, MA: Massachusetts Division of Fisheries and Wildlife.

Paulson, D. R. and S. W. Dunkle. 1999. *A Checklist of North American Odonata.* Tacoma, WA: Slater Museum of Natural History, University of Puget Sound, Occasional Paper #56.

Rosche, L. 2002. *Dragonflies and Damselflies of Northeast Ohio.* Cleveland, OH: Cleveland Museum of Natural History.

Shaw, J. 1987. *John Shaw's Closeups in Nature.* New York, NY: Amphoto.

Walker, E. M., and P. S. Corbet. 1975. *The Odonata of Canada and Alaska, Volume 1.* Toronto, ON: Univ. Toronto Press.

West, L., and J. Ridl 1994. *How to Photograph Insects and Spiders.* Mechanicsburg, PA: Stackpole Books.

Westfall, M. J. and M. L. May. 1996. *Damselflies of North America.* Gainesville, FL: Scientific Publishers.

Appendix E

Binoculars for "Damselflying"

Quality close-focusing optics have opened the door to the hobby of damselfly watching or "damselflying." Close-focusing is a must; full-size is preferable; power is a matter of choice. Listed here is a sampling of the best binoculars for watching our "fair damsels."

Weight is listed because some folks prefer lighter optics. The compact binoculars are lighter, but they gather less light at dawn and dusk. They are also harder to hold steady than their full-size cousins. Compacts are nice for easy packing on longer hikes.

Good damselflying binoculars should focus under ten feet and preferably under six feet. This gives you the magnification to better fill your field-of-view with the damselfly.

The last column represents relative brightness. The higher the number the brighter your view will be. This is important for picking out details at dawn and dusk. Though brightness is not as big a deal as it is with birding binoculars, some damselflies do fly at dusk when a brighter view would be a bonus.

What is the difference between 10-power and 8-power? With increased power one loses brightness. As stated above, this may not be a big problem with dragonflying. Also with higher power binoculars, any body movement is magnified.

Brand	size	weight (in oz.)	closest focus (ft.)	brightness
Bausch & Lomb				
8x42 WP Elite	full-size	29	5	28
10x42 WP Elite	full-size	28	5	18
7x26 Custom	compact	13	6	14
10x42 WP Discoverer	full-size	30	8	18
8x24 Legacy	compact	8	8	9
Brunton				
7.5x43 Epoch	full-size	25	3	28
10.5x43 Epoch	full-size	25	3	18
7x42 Eterna	full-size	34	5.5	28
10x42 Eterna	full-size	34	6	18
Bushnell				
8x42 Legend	full-size	30	6	28
10x42 Legend	full-size	30	6	18

Brand	size	weight (in oz.)	closest focus	brightness
Eagle				
8x42 Ranger PC	full-size	23	5.2	28
10x42 Ranger PC	full-size	23	5.2	18
6x32 Ranger Platinum	full-size	19	3	28
8x32 Ranger Platinum	full-size	19	3	14
Kahles				
8x42 DCF	full-size	26	8	28
10x42 DCF	full-size	26	8	18
8x32 DCF	full-size	22	5	14
Leica				
8x32 BN Ultra	full-size	22	7	16
10x32 Trinovid Ultra	full-size	24	7	10
Minox				
8x32 BD/BR	full-size	22	5	16
10x42 BD/BR	full-size	27	8	16
Nikon				
8x20 Venturer LX	compact	10	8	9
8x32 Venturer LX	full-size	25	8	16
8x42 Venturer LX	full-size	35	9	28
8x42 Monarch ATB/PC	full-size	21	8	28
Pentax				
8x32 DCF WP	full-size	23	7	16
8x42 DCF WP	full-size	27	8	28
10x42 DCF WP	full-size	27	9	18
10x24 UCF MC	compact	12	7	6
Swarovski				
8x20 B/G	compact	8	8	6
8.5x42 EL	full-size	29	8	24
10x42 EL	full-size	28	8	18
Swift				
7x36 Eaglet WP	full-size	21	5	26
10x42 Viceroy WP	full-size	24	6	18
8x25 Trilyte	compact	14	8	9
10x25 Trilyte	compact	14	8	6
Zeiss				
10x40 Victory	full-size	26	8	16

Index

Field Notes

Field Notes

Field Notes

Field Notes